Casting Conquests: The Surprising Runner-Ups for Iconic Roles

Michael Pollick

Published by Michael Pollick, 2024.

While every precaution has been taken in the preparation of this book, the publisher assumes no responsibility for errors or omissions, or for damages resulting from the use of the information contained herein.

CASTING CONQUESTS: THE SURPRISING RUNNER-UPS FOR ICONIC ROLES

First edition. September 10, 2024.

Copyright © 2024 Michael Pollick.

ISBN: 979-8224072514

Written by Michael Pollick.

Table of Contents

Casting Conquests: The Surprising Runner-Ups for Iconic Roles

Michael Pollick

Time-Traveling Casting Decisions: How "Back to the Future" Became a Classic

When we think of iconic films, "Back to the Future" often springs to mind, a timeless classic that has transcended generations. But what if I told you that the casting choices that eventually brought Marty McFly and Doc Brown to life were not the original ones envisioned by the filmmakers? Yes, the journey to the final cast was filled with twists and turns, much like the time-traveling DeLorean itself.

First, let's talk about Marty McFly, the teenager who inadvertently becomes a time traveler. The role was initially offered to a young actor named Eric Stoltz. Stoltz was a rising star in the early 1980s, known for his serious roles and dramatic chops. He was cast after an extensive audition process, and filming began with him in the lead. However, as production progressed, director Robert Zemeckis and producer Steven Spielberg realized that Stoltz's portrayal wasn't quite fitting the light-hearted, comedic tone they envisioned for the film. They found Stoltz's performance too intense for a character that needed to be relatable and fun. After several weeks of shooting, they made the tough decision to recast the role.

Enter Michael J. Fox, the actor who would become synonymous with the character of Marty McFly. Fox was initially unavailable due to his commitment to the television series "Family Ties." But the filmmakers were relentless in their pursuit of the right fit for the role. They were captivated by Fox's charm and comedic timing, and they were determined to find a way to get him on board. After much negotiation, Fox agreed to take on the role, filming "Back to the Future" during the day and returning to "Family Ties" at night. This grueling schedule showcased his dedication and talent, and it ultimately paid off. Fox's performance brought an infectious energy to Marty, capturing the essence of a teenager caught in extraordinary circumstances.

Now, let's shift gears to the eccentric scientist, Dr. Emmett Brown. Originally, the role was offered to the legendary actor John Lithgow. Lithgow was known for his versatility and ability to bring depth to his characters, but he ultimately turned down the role. This opened the door for Christopher Lloyd, who brought a unique blend of eccentricity and warmth to Doc Brown. Lloyd's portrayal became iconic, with his wild hair and expressive mannerisms defining the character. He infused Doc with a sense of urgency and mad genius that resonated with audiences, making him one of the most memorable characters in cinematic history.

It's fascinating to consider how different the film might have been had Stoltz and Lithgow remained in their roles. Would "Back to the Future" have achieved the same level of success? Would it have become the cultural phenomenon it is today? The chemistry between Fox and Lloyd is undeniable, and it's hard to imagine anyone else in those roles. Their performances contributed significantly to the film's charm and humor, making it a beloved classic.

As we delve deeper into the casting choices, we discover that the film's success was not just about the leads. The supporting cast also played crucial roles. For instance, the character of George McFly, Marty's father, was originally offered to actor Hugh Laurie, who would later gain fame for his role in "House." Laurie turned it down, and the role eventually went to Crispin Glover, whose quirky portrayal added an extra layer of depth to the character.

In retrospect, the casting decisions made during the production of "Back to the Future" were pivotal. They shaped the film into the beloved classic it is today. The journey from initial casting choices to the final product is a testament to the importance of finding the right actors for the right roles. It reminds us that sometimes, the best stories come from unexpected turns, much like the adventures of Marty and Doc as they navigate the complexities of time travel.

The Casting Conundrum: How Al Pacino, James Caan, and Diane Keaton Became the Faces of The Godfather

When we think about iconic films, few resonate as deeply as Francis Ford Coppola's "The Godfather." Released in 1972, it has become a cornerstone of American cinema, a film that not only defined a genre but also reshaped the landscape of storytelling on the silver screen. However, what many may not realize is that the path to casting the legendary roles of Don Vito Corleone, Michael Corleone, and the rest of the Corleone family was fraught with controversy, uncertainty, and a series of surprising choices that could have changed the film's legacy entirely.

Let's start with the role of Don Vito Corleone, originally envisioned for the legendary actor, Marlon Brando. But Brando wasn't the first choice. In fact, the production team initially considered several actors, including the powerhouse performance of George C. Scott. Scott was known for his intense portrayals and could have brought a different energy to the character. However, he ultimately turned down the role, leading the casting team to look elsewhere. Another name that floated around was the esteemed actor, Laurence Olivier, who, despite his talent, was deemed too British for the Italian-American patriarch. The search continued until Brando, who had a reputation for being difficult, was finally approached. His unconventional audition—where he famously stuffed his cheeks with cotton balls to create the character's unique appearance—was a gamble that paid off. Brando's portrayal became legendary, earning him an Academy Award for Best Actor, but it was a role that almost went to someone else entirely.

Then there's Michael Corleone, the character that would catapult Al Pacino into superstardom. Interestingly, Pacino was not the first choice for this pivotal role either. The producers initially considered a range of actors, including the handsome and charismatic Robert Redford. Redford, with his all-American looks, could have brought a different dynamic to the character, but he was ultimately deemed too clean-cut to embody the complexities of Michael's transformation from the family outsider to a ruthless mob boss. Other contenders included Jack Nicholson, who was on the rise but still somewhat of a wild card. It wasn't until Pacino, who had only a handful of roles under his belt, auditioned for the part that the team began to see the potential in him. He brought a vulnerability to Michael that was essential to the character's arc, and his performance became one of the film's most memorable elements.

Let's not forget about the character of Sonny Corleone, Michael's hot-headed older brother. Initially, the role was offered to James Caan, but he wasn't the first choice either. The producers had considered actors like Ryan O'Neal and even Burt Reynolds. Reynolds, with his charisma and rugged good looks, seemed like a natural fit, yet he turned it down, believing the role wouldn't be a good match for him. Caan, however, brought a raw intensity to Sonny that was crucial to the film's emotional weight. His portrayal of the impulsive and fiery son became one of the standout performances, showcasing the inner turmoil of a man caught between loyalty and violence.

As for the character of Kay Adams, Michael's love interest, the role was initially offered to a variety of actresses, including the talented but lesser-known actress, Jennifer O'Neill. Ultimately, Diane Keaton was cast, and her portrayal brought a unique blend of strength and vulnerability that resonated with audiences. Keaton's chemistry with

Pacino became one of the film's defining relationships, adding depth to Michael's character and his eventual descent into the world of crime.

In retrospect, it's fascinating to consider how different "The Godfather" might have been had these original casting choices come to fruition. The film is a masterpiece not only because of its direction and writing but also due to the iconic performances that shaped its legacy. Each actor brought something unique to their role, and the chemistry between them created a tapestry of familial loyalty, betrayal, and power that continues to captivate audiences. The casting decisions, often seen as mere footnotes in the film's history, are, in fact, crucial to understanding the magic that is "The Godfather."

Exploring the Alternate Stars who Almost Stepped into the Iconic Roles of "One Flew Over the Cuckoo's Nest"

When we think of "One Flew Over the Cuckoo's Nest," it's hard not to envision Jack Nicholson's iconic portrayal of Randle P. McMurphy. His performance is so deeply ingrained in the fabric of the film that it's almost impossible to imagine anyone else in that role. But what if I told you that the casting process for this seminal film was a labyrinth of choices, rejections, and near-misses that could have led to an entirely different cinematic experience? The original casting choices reveal a fascinating glimpse into the film industry of the 1970s, the creative vision of director Milos Forman, and the unpredictable nature of Hollywood.

Originally, the role of McMurphy was offered to several actors before Nicholson stepped into the limelight. Among them was the legendary actor, Burt Reynolds, who, at the time, was riding high on a wave of popularity. Reynolds had the charisma and the rugged charm that could have brought a different energy to the character. However, he ultimately turned down the role, a decision that would change the course of cinematic history. Imagine a world where Reynolds, with his devil-may-care attitude, was the one leading the charge against the oppressive forces of the mental institution. It's a tantalizing thought, but ultimately, it was Nicholson's raw intensity that made McMurphy a symbol of rebellion.

Then there was the intriguing choice of Gene Hackman, another heavyweight of American cinema. Hackman, known for his versatility and depth, was considered for the role, and one can only wonder how his nuanced approach might have reshaped McMurphy's character. Hackman's ability to oscillate between vulnerability and strength could have added layers to the role. However, he too passed on the opportunity, leaving the door wide open for Nicholson, who infused the character with a manic energy that resonated with audiences and critics alike.

While McMurphy's casting journey was a rollercoaster, the character of Nurse Ratched also had her share of potential candidates. The formidable Louise Fletcher ultimately brought Nurse Ratched to life, earning an Academy Award for her performance. But initially, the role was offered to several actresses, including Anne Bancroft, who was already an established star thanks to her work in "The Graduate." Bancroft had the gravitas and the presence that could have made Nurse Ratched a chilling adversary. However, she also declined the role, which opened the door for Fletcher to deliver a performance that would haunt viewers for decades.

It's also worth mentioning the casting of other pivotal characters in the film. The role of Chief Bromden, the towering figure who narrates the story, was nearly filled by a different actor. The filmmakers considered a range of options, including the talented actor, George C. Scott. Scott's powerful presence could have brought a different dynamic to the character, but he too was not meant to be. It was ultimately Will Sampson, a Native American actor and member of the Creek Nation, who embodied the role with a quiet strength that resonated deeply with audiences.

The casting choices for "One Flew Over the Cuckoo's Nest" highlight the unpredictable nature of filmmaking. Each actor brought their own unique interpretation and energy to the table, and it's fascinating to ponder how different the film might have been with any of those original choices. The alchemy of performances, the direction, and the screenplay all converged to create a masterpiece that stands the test of time. It's a reminder that behind every iconic film lies a complex tapestry of decisions, where the right choice at the right moment can lead to something extraordinary. In the end, while we celebrate Nicholson and Fletcher for their unforgettable roles, we also acknowledge the myriad of actors whose paths diverged from this project, each leaving their own mark on the legacy of cinema.

What If Gary Sinise Were Forrest Gump?

The Original Casting Choices That Could Have BeenWhen we think about the iconic film "Forrest Gump," it's hard to separate the character from the actor who portrayed him, Tom Hanks. Hanks became synonymous with the role, delivering a performance that not only won him an Academy Award but also etched Forrest Gump into the annals of cinematic history. However, the path to casting this beloved character was anything but straightforward. The original casting choices provide a fascinating glimpse into the behind-the-scenes decisions that shaped this classic film.

Initially, the role of Forrest Gump was offered to John Travolta, who was at the height of his fame following his success in films like "Saturday Night Fever" and "Pulp Fiction." Travolta was intrigued by the script and the character's unique journey, but ultimately, he turned it down. It's interesting to think about how different the film might have been with Travolta's charm and charisma infusing the character. Would Forrest Gump have had the same whimsical innocence? Would his journey through American history have resonated as deeply?

After Travolta, the role was considered for other notable actors, including Bill Murray and Chevy Chase. Both were comedic heavyweights in the 1990s, and their involvement could have shifted the tone of the film. Imagine Bill Murray's dry wit or Chevy Chase's slapstick humor applied to the character of Forrest. The film might have leaned more heavily into comedy, potentially losing the poignant undertones that made it so impactful.

As the casting process continued, the filmmakers also looked at actors like Steve Martin and even the up-and-coming actor Matthew McConaughey, who had not yet reached the stardom he would later achieve. McConaughey's laid-back persona could have brought a different flavor to Forrest, perhaps making him more of a cool, easy-going character rather than the earnest, sweet-natured man we came to love.

Interestingly, the casting team also considered actors who were not mainstream stars at the time. One such actor was Gary Sinise, who eventually found his way into the film as Lieutenant Dan. Sinise had the chops to bring depth to the character, but it's curious to ponder what might have happened if he had taken on the role of Forrest instead. Would he have been able to convey the same level of innocence and simplicity that Hanks delivered?

As the search continued, the filmmakers were beginning to feel the pressure of finding the right actor. It was during this time that Tom Hanks, who had already established himself as a formidable talent with films like "Big" and "Philadelphia," expressed interest in the role. Hanks had a unique ability to embody characters with a deep sense of humanity, and that was exactly what Forrest Gump needed.

When Hanks finally got the role, it was a match made in cinematic heaven. His portrayal was not just about the character's quirks and catchphrases; it was about bringing to life a man who, despite his challenges, saw the world through a lens of hope and determination. Hanks infused Forrest with a sense of authenticity that resonated with audiences around the globe.

Looking back, it's easy to see how the casting choices could have dramatically altered the film's trajectory. The chemistry between Hanks and Robin Wright, who played Jenny, was integral to the film's emotional core. Hanks' ability to portray vulnerability and sincerity allowed viewers to connect deeply with Forrest's journey.

Ultimately, while the casting process for "Forrest Gump" included several big names and promising talents, it was Tom Hanks who became the heart and soul of the film. The original casting choices remind us that sometimes, the best decisions are the ones we never see coming, leading to a masterpiece that continues to touch hearts and inspire generations.

"Behind the Curtain: Uncovering the Complexities of Casting in 'Gone With the Wind'"

When we think of classic cinema, few films resonate as deeply as "Gone With The Wind." Released in 1939, it has become a cultural touchstone, a sweeping epic that encapsulates the tumultuous era of the American South during the Civil War and Reconstruction. But behind the glamour and grandeur of the film lies a fascinating story of casting decisions that could have dramatically altered its legacy. The original casting choices for "Gone With The Wind" are a testament to the complexities of Hollywood during that time, revealing not just the desires of filmmakers but also the cultural attitudes and expectations of an entire nation.

Initially, the role of Scarlett O'Hara, the headstrong Southern belle at the heart of the story, was a coveted part that attracted many prominent actresses of the day. Among the first contenders was the iconic actress Bette Davis. Known for her fierce performances and strong screen presence, Davis seemed like a natural fit for the role. However, she had her own reservations about the character, believing Scarlett to be unlikable and morally ambiguous. This self-awareness led her to decline the role, paving the way for others to audition.

Another early favorite was Katharine Hepburn, whose talent and charisma were undeniable. Yet, the producers were concerned that Hepburn's strong-willed persona would overshadow the character's inherent vulnerability. In the end, the search for the perfect Scarlett continued, leading to a nationwide talent hunt that became a media spectacle. The casting director, David O. Selznick, received thousands of letters from hopeful actresses, each vying for the chance to embody this complex character.

As the search intensified, the name of Vivien Leigh emerged. A British actress relatively unknown in America at the time, Leigh's audition was nothing short of electrifying. She captured the essence of Scarlett with a blend of ferocity and fragility that left a lasting impression on Selznick. However, her casting wasn't without controversy. Many in Hollywood questioned whether an English actress could authentically portray a quintessentially Southern character. Yet, Selznick was undeterred, convinced that Leigh was the embodiment of Scarlett's spirit.

On the other side of the casting spectrum was the role of Rhett Butler, the charming and roguish hero who captures Scarlett's heart. The part was initially offered to a string of actors, including Gary Cooper and Clark Gable. Cooper, known for his rugged good looks, ultimately turned it down, believing that the character lacked depth. It was Gable, however, who would ultimately claim the role, despite initial reluctance from Selznick, who feared Gable's off-screen persona might overshadow the character. Gable's portrayal would go on to define Rhett Butler, cementing his place in cinematic history.

The casting choices extended beyond the leads as well. The role of Mammy, Scarlett's loyal servant, was another point of contention. Hattie McDaniel, a talented actress and singer, was eventually cast, but not without significant challenges. The film's portrayal of African American characters faced scrutiny, and McDaniel herself encountered racial prejudice in Hollywood. Despite this, her performance earned her an Academy Award for Best Supporting Actress, making her the first African American to win an Oscar. This moment was both a triumph and a reminder of the complexities surrounding race in American cinema.

As "Gone With The Wind" premiered, it became a monumental success, but the original casting choices remain a significant part of its narrative. The film's legacy, intertwined with the stories of those who almost played its characters, illustrates the intricate dance of talent, timing, and societal expectations. It invites us to reflect not only on the performances that graced the screen but also on the cultural context that shaped them. The casting decisions for "Gone With The Wind" remind us that behind every iconic film is a rich tapestry of stories, aspirations, and the ever-evolving landscape of Hollywood.

The Near-Misses: Why Frank Sinatra, Steve McQueen, and Robert Mitchum Almost Starred in "Dirty Harry"

When we think of iconic films, "Dirty Harry" often springs to mind, not just for its gritty portrayal of crime and justice, but also for the unforgettable performance of Clint Eastwood as Inspector Harry Callahan. However, the path to casting this legendary role was fraught with interesting twists and turns that reveal much about the film industry in the early 1970s. The original casting choices for "Dirty Harry" provide a fascinating glimpse into how the film might have diverged from the classic we know today.

Initially, the role of Harry Callahan was envisioned for a different actor altogether. Before Eastwood was brought on board, the filmmakers considered several prominent names, including Frank Sinatra. Yes, the same man whose smooth voice and charm captivated audiences in the 1960s. Sinatra was a huge star at the time, and the idea of him playing a tough, no-nonsense cop was intriguing. However, the project faced a significant hurdle when Sinatra's commitment to the film "The Detective" conflicted with the shooting schedule for "Dirty Harry." Ultimately, the scheduling issues led to Sinatra stepping away from the role, which opened the door for other actors.

In addition to Sinatra, another name that emerged in discussions was Steve McQueen. McQueen was the quintessential anti-hero of the era, known for his rugged good looks and brooding charisma. The producers saw him as a potential fit for the role, given his ability to embody a tough, rebellious spirit. However, McQueen had his own demands regarding the character's portrayal and the film's direction. He wanted more creative control, including the ability to shape Harry Callahan's personality to align with his own vision. The negotiations proved to be complicated, and ultimately, McQueen opted out, leaving the role vacant once again.

With these high-profile actors stepping aside, the search for the right fit continued. The next name that surfaced was Robert Mitchum, a veteran actor with a long-standing reputation for playing gritty roles. Mitchum had a certain gravitas that could have brought a different flavor to Callahan, but he was also seen as too old for the character as envisioned by the filmmakers. The role required a young, dynamic presence, someone who could embody the raw energy and intensity of the streets of San Francisco. Mitchum's age and established persona meant he would have been a mismatch for the film's tone.

As the casting process evolved, the filmmakers began to look at a broader range of actors, including those who were not yet household names. They considered actors like Burt Lancaster and even the young Al Pacino, who was just beginning to make a name for himself in Hollywood. However, none of these options seemed to fit the bill. It was during this tumultuous search that Clint Eastwood entered the picture. Eastwood, who had already gained fame from his role in the "Dollars Trilogy" and the television series "Rawhide," was seen as a fresh choice. His rugged demeanor and ability to convey a sense of moral ambiguity made him an ideal candidate for the role of Harry Callahan.

When Eastwood finally stepped into the shoes of Dirty Harry, it was as if the character had been waiting for him all along. His performance was electric, combining a tough exterior with a complex inner turmoil that resonated with audiences. The film became a cultural touchstone, and Eastwood's portrayal of the unyielding cop solidified his status as a Hollywood icon.

Looking back, it's fascinating to consider how different "Dirty Harry" might have been had Sinatra, McQueen, or Mitchum taken on the role. Each actor brought their own unique style and interpretation, which could have shifted the film's narrative and legacy entirely. Ultimately, Clint Eastwood's casting was not just a fortunate decision; it was a pivotal moment in cinematic history, reminding us that sometimes the stars align in unexpected ways.

The Fascinating Alternatives to John Travolta and Olivia Newton-John in Grease

When we think of "Grease," we often picture the iconic performances of John Travolta and Olivia Newton-John, their chemistry lighting up the screen as Danny and Sandy. But what if I told you that the casting choices for this beloved musical could have been entirely different? The film, which premiered in 1978, has become a cultural touchstone, but the road to casting was filled with unexpected turns and fascinating alternatives that might have changed the face of the film entirely.

Originally, the role of Danny Zuko was offered to several actors before Travolta stepped into the spotlight. Among those considered was Henry Winkler, who was riding high on the success of "Happy Days." Imagine if Winkler, known for his portrayal of the lovable but tough Arthur "The Fonz" Fonzarelli, had taken on the role of the greaser with a heart. His charm and charisma could have brought a different flavor to the character, but would he have delivered the same electrifying dance moves that Travolta is famous for? It's hard to say. Another name tossed around was Jeff Conaway, who eventually played Kenickie in the film. Conaway had initially auditioned for Danny, and his dynamic presence might have added a different energy to the film.

As for Sandy Olsson, the sweet Australian exchange student who captures Danny's heart, the casting choices were equally intriguing. Before Olivia Newton-John was cast, the producers considered a slew of actresses, including Carrie Fisher, who was fresh off her success as

Princess Leia in "Star Wars." Fisher's sharp wit and strong presence could have transformed Sandy into a more assertive character. The juxtaposition of her fierce personality against Travolta's charming rogue would have created a unique dynamic, but would it have resonated with audiences in the same way?

Interestingly, the role of Rizzo, the tough yet vulnerable leader of the Pink Ladies, was almost filled by a different actress as well. Stockard Channing's portrayal is now iconic, but Bette Midler was initially considered for the role. Midler, known for her brassy, bold performances, could have infused Rizzo with a more comedic edge. While Channing brought depth and nuance to Rizzo's character, Midler's version might have leaned into the humor, making Rizzo a more overtly comedic character.

The casting of the supporting characters also had its share of surprises. For example, the role of Doody, the sweet-natured guitarist, was originally thought to be a good fit for a young actor named Michael Lembeck, who later went on to direct "The New Adventures of Old Christine." Lembeck's youthful charm could have made Doody a standout character, but ultimately, it was Barry Pearl who brought a delightful innocence to the role.

And let's not forget about the legendary role of the Teen Angel, played by Frankie Avalon in the film. Avalon's smooth, nostalgic performance was a perfect fit for the dreamy sequence, but initially, the producers explored the possibility of casting someone like Bobby Vinton. Vinton, known for his romantic ballads, could have brought a different musical style to the role, perhaps leaning more into the crooning tradition of the era.

Ultimately, the casting of "Grease" shaped not only the film but also the cultural landscape of the late 1970s. The choices made during the casting process contributed to the film's enduring legacy, creating a timeless classic that continues to resonate with audiences today. It's fascinating to ponder how different actors might have interpreted these roles, how their unique talents could have altered the film's trajectory. Would we still be singing along to "Summer Nights" or "You're the One That I Want" if the casting choices had been different? The magic of "Grease" lies not just in its catchy songs and vibrant dance numbers but also in the serendipity of its casting, a perfect storm that brought together the right people at the right time.

The Rise and Fall of Stardom: How Casting Choices in "A Star Is Born" Reflect the Evolution of Hollywood

In the landscape of cinema, few stories have been retold as often as "A Star Is Born." This tale, which weaves the rise of a hopeful star with the tragic decline of a seasoned artist, has captivated audiences since its inception. Yet, what often goes unnoticed in the glimmer of its iconic performances are the casting choices that could have shaped the film differently. The original casting decisions for the various adaptations of "A Star Is Born" reveal a fascinating tapestry of what could have been, a glimpse into the labyrinth of Hollywood's creative process.

The film's journey began in 1937, originally starring Janet Gaynor and Fredric March. At that time, Gaynor was a celebrated actress, known for her emotional depth and ability to evoke empathy. March, with his commanding presence and nuanced performances, was an ideal choice for the tortured artist. However, the casting process for later adaptations would reveal an array of potential stars who were considered, each bringing their own unique flair to the roles.

Fast forward to the 1976 version, which introduced Barbra Streisand and Kris Kristofferson to a new generation. Streisand was a force of nature, her voice powerful enough to fill any room, and her ability to convey vulnerability made her a perfect fit for Esther Hoffman. The chemistry between her and Kristofferson, who was a rising star with his rugged charm and musical talent, created a dynamic that resonated with audiences. Yet, before Streisand was chosen, other names floated around the casting table. There was talk of Liza Minnelli, whose own star was on the rise, and even Diana Ross, who was considered for her vocal prowess and screen presence.

Imagine, for a moment, if Minnelli had taken on the role. Her theatrical background and flair for dramatic expression could have brought a different energy to the film, one steeped in the vibrancy of the 1970s. Or consider the impact of Diana Ross, who, with her iconic status and soulful voice, would have infused the character with a distinct rhythm and gravitas. The creative team ultimately settled on Streisand, but the potential paths not taken linger in the air, like an unfinished melody.

As we shift to the most recent remake, released in 2018, the casting choices once again sparked conversation. The film featured Lady Gaga and Bradley Cooper, a pairing that seemed almost destined. Gaga, with her multifaceted talent as a singer and actress, brought an authenticity to Ally that resonated deeply with audiences. Cooper, who directed the film as well, embodied the tortured artist Jackson Maine with a raw intensity that felt both personal and universal. However, prior to their casting, other names were considered.

There were whispers of Beyoncé stepping into the role of Ally, a choice that would have undoubtedly shifted the film's cultural landscape. Her star power and musical background could have created a different narrative, one that might have leaned more heavily into themes of empowerment and resilience. Similarly, the idea of actors like Tom Hardy or even Ryan Gosling as Jackson Maine was floated, each bringing their own interpretations to the character. Hardy's rugged intensity could have provided a darker, grittier portrayal, while Gosling's charm might have added a more romantic layer to the story.

The evolution of casting choices in "A Star Is Born" reflects not just the changing tides of Hollywood, but also the shifting sensibilities of audiences. Each iteration of the film has brought forth unique interpretations and performances that resonate with the cultural context of their time. The original casting choices, the names that were considered, and the paths that were not taken all contribute to the rich history of this beloved story, reminding us that the magic of cinema lies not just in the final product, but in the journey of creation and the myriad possibilities that exist within it.

"Show-Stopping Secrets: The Surprising Casting Decisions Behind 'Little Shop of Horrors'"

When we think about the cult classic "Little Shop of Horrors," we often envision the vibrant characters, the catchy tunes, and that unmistakable blend of horror and humor. But behind the scenes, the casting choices for this film adaptation were as colorful and complex as the story itself. Originally conceived as a low-budget musical in the early 1980s, "Little Shop of Horrors" found its way to the big screen in 1986, but the journey to casting the right actors was anything but straightforward.

Initially, the role of Seymour Krelborn, the meek and lovable protagonist, was a hot topic of discussion. The creators had their eyes on several actors, but one name that frequently surfaced was that of the talented and versatile actor, Rick Moranis. Moranis, known for his work in comedies like "Ghostbusters" and "Spaceballs," ultimately became the face of Seymour, bringing an endearing quality to the character that resonated with audiences. But it's interesting to note that before Moranis was secured, other actors were considered, including the likes of Robert Downey Jr. and even a young Nicolas Cage. Can you imagine a world where Cage, with his intense and unpredictable energy, stepped into the role of the timid florist? It's a fascinating thought, but ultimately, Moranis's charm and comedic timing made him the perfect fit.

And then there's Audrey, Seymour's love interest, a character that needed to embody both vulnerability and a certain tragic allure. The original choice for Audrey was none other than Ellen Greene, who had originated the role in the off-Broadway production. Greene's unique voice and quirky charm made her a standout, and her transition to the film was seamless. However, the producers also toyed with the idea of casting other big names, including the likes of Madonna and even a then-rising star, Jennifer Jason Leigh. Imagine the impact Madonna's star power could have had on the film, but perhaps Greene's soulful rendition of "Somewhere That's Green" would have been lost in the shuffle of celebrity.

Now, let's talk about the infamous plant, Audrey II. This character was not just a puppet but a pivotal force in the narrative, demanding a voice that could encapsulate both menace and charisma. Initially, the role was envisioned for a variety of performers, including the legendary voice of James Earl Jones. Can you picture the deep, resonant tones of Jones echoing through the theater as he delivered the plant's lines? It would have added an entirely different layer of gravitas to the character. But ultimately, the role went to Levi Stubbs, the lead singer of The Four Tops, whose soulful and powerful voice gave Audrey II a personality that was both charming and terrifying. Stubbs's performance was so memorable that it's hard to imagine anyone else filling those shoes.

As for the supporting characters, the casting process was equally intriguing. The role of Mushnik, Seymour's boss, was initially offered to a few notable actors, including the beloved comedian, Jerry Stiller. However, it was Vincent Gardenia who ultimately brought the character to life, providing a perfect blend of gruffness and humor. The film also featured a standout performance by Steve Martin as the sadistic dentist Orin Scrivello, a role that Martin embraced with his trademark comedic flair. Interestingly, the filmmakers had also considered other actors, such as Bill Murray, who would have undoubtedly brought his own unique style to the character.

In retrospect, the casting choices for "Little Shop of Horrors" shaped the film into the beloved classic it is today. Each actor brought their own unique essence to their roles, creating a tapestry of performances that resonated with audiences. The original vision may have included a variety of names, but it was the final choices that captured the heart and humor of the story, leaving an indelible mark on musical cinema. The film became a celebration of talent, creativity, and the unexpected twists that come with bringing a story to life.

The Cast That Almost Was: Surprising Casting Choices Behind the Iconic M*A*S*H

When we think about the iconic film M*A*S*H, it's hard not to picture the ensemble cast that brought the characters to life, but what many don't realize is that the casting process for this groundbreaking movie was anything but straightforward. The film, released in 1970 and directed by Robert Altman, is based on the novel by Richard Hooker and set during the Korean War, but its irreverent humor and anti-establishment themes resonated deeply with the social upheaval of the time, particularly the Vietnam War. The casting choices were pivotal in shaping the film's tone, yet the original selections were quite different from what audiences ultimately saw on screen.

Initially, the role of Hawkeye Pierce, the charmingly cynical lead character, was offered to none other than the legendary actor, Jack Nicholson. At that time, Nicholson was gaining recognition for his roles in films like Easy Rider and Five Easy Pieces, and he seemed like a natural fit for the part. However, as fate would have it, Nicholson turned down the role, believing that the character was too similar to his previous portrayals. This decision opened the door for Alan Alda, who would go on to define Hawkeye's character with his unique blend of humor and depth. Alda's performance became a cornerstone of the film and the subsequent television series, but it's fascinating to consider how Nicholson's interpretation might have altered the film's legacy.

Similarly, the role of Trapper John McIntyre was initially offered to a variety of actors before settling on Elliott Gould. Among those considered were the likes of Donald Sutherland, who ultimately took on the role. Gould's portrayal brought a laid-back, almost whimsical quality to Trapper John, contrasting beautifully with Alda's more intense Hawkeye. It's interesting to think about the chemistry between the two leads; Gould's comedic timing and improvisational skills complemented Alda's more serious undertones. The casting of Gould was a stroke of genius, as he embodied the free-spirited nature of the character, making the duo one of the most memorable partnerships in film history.

Then there was the character of Hot Lips Houlihan, who was originally intended to be played by Anne Bancroft, a celebrated actress known for her roles in The Graduate and The Miracle Worker. However, Bancroft's commitment to other projects meant she had to decline. Instead, the role went to Sally Kellerman, who brought a unique blend of vulnerability and strength to the character. Kellerman's Hot Lips became a symbol of the film's feminist undertones, showcasing a woman who was both a capable leader and a complex individual. The casting shift not only changed the character's trajectory but also highlighted the evolving roles of women in cinema during that era.

The casting for the film extended beyond the leads; even supporting roles were subject to interesting changes. For instance, the character of Frank Burns was initially thought to be played by actor Bob Newhart, known for his deadpan humor. However, the role ultimately went to Larry Linville, whose portrayal of the pompous and insecure surgeon became one of the film's highlights. Linville's ability to balance comedy with a certain pathos made Frank Burns a memorable antagonist, and it's hard to imagine anyone else in that role.

What's striking about the casting of M*A*S*H is how the original choices reflect the cultural landscape of the time. The film was a bold commentary on war, authority, and the absurdity of life, and the actors who ultimately filled those roles were instrumental in conveying that message. Each casting decision influenced not just the film itself but also the wider cultural conversation surrounding it. The original casting choices, while intriguing, ultimately paved the way for a film that would become a classic, resonating with audiences for decades. The legacy of M*A*S*H is not just in its story or its humor, but in how these actors, through their performances, captured the spirit of a generation grappling with the complexities of war and identity.

Titanic's Forgotten Casting Choices: The Roles That Almost Went to Matthew McConaughey and Gwyneth Paltrow

When we think of the iconic film "Titanic," our minds immediately conjure images of Jack and Rose, played by Leonardo DiCaprio and Kate Winslet, navigating the tumultuous waters of love and tragedy aboard the ill-fated ship. However, the path to casting these two stars was anything but straightforward. The original casting choices reveal a fascinating glimpse into the world of Hollywood, where almost every role has its own set of potential actors, each bringing a unique flavor to the characters they might portray.

Initially, when James Cameron began piecing together his vision for "Titanic," he had a different set of actors in mind. In fact, the casting process was extensive, with a range of actors auditioning for the roles of Jack Dawson and Rose DeWitt Bukater. One of the most notable names that surfaced during the early stages was Matthew McConaughey. At that time, McConaughey was on the rise, having just gained attention for his role in "Dazed and Confused." His charm and charisma made him a strong contender for the role of Jack, but ultimately, Cameron felt that DiCaprio embodied the youthful innocence and longing that Jack required.

On the other side, Rose was initially envisioned with a different actress entirely. Cameron had considered Gwyneth Paltrow, who was also gaining traction in Hollywood. Paltrow had that ethereal quality that could easily represent the upper-class young woman trapped in a world of expectations and societal norms. However, as the casting process unfolded, Kate Winslet emerged as the front-runner. Winslet brought a raw, authentic energy to Rose that resonated deeply with Cameron's vision. Her audition was a turning point; she portrayed Rose's complexity, her strength, and her vulnerability in a way that captivated everyone involved.

Interestingly, the casting choices didn't stop at the lead roles. The supporting cast was equally intriguing, with several A-list actors considered for pivotal roles. For example, the role of Cal Hockley, Rose's wealthy fiancé, was initially eyed by a different set of actors, including Billy Zane, who would eventually land the role. However, before Zane was cast, actors like Josh Lucas and even the charismatic Jude Law were in the mix. It's fascinating to think about how different the dynamic of the film could have been with a different Cal, but Zane's portrayal added a layer of complexity to the character, making him both charming and menacing.

Moreover, the role of Molly Brown, the unsinkable character portrayed by Kathy Bates, had its own set of casting possibilities. Originally, Cameron had considered a variety of actresses, including the likes of Bette Midler. Midler's larger-than-life persona could have brought a different energy to the role, but Bates ultimately delivered a performance that was both heartwarming and empowering, capturing the essence of the real-life figure who became a symbol of resilience and strength.

The casting choices for "Titanic" reflect not just the actors' talents but also the vision that Cameron had for the film. Each actor brought their own interpretation to the table, and the chemistry between the leads was crucial. The film's success hinged on the believable connection between Jack and Rose, and it's remarkable to consider how different the film might have been with any of the alternate casting choices.

In the end, while the casting process was filled with potential and possibilities, it ultimately led to a pairing that would become iconic in cinematic history. DiCaprio and Winslet not only defined their characters but also created a legacy that would resonate for generations. Their performances, set against the backdrop of one of the most tragic maritime disasters, became a cultural touchstone, reminding us that sometimes, the stars align perfectly, even when the journey to get there is fraught with uncertainty.

The Unseen Force: Behind-the-Scenes Insights into the Casting of A New Hope

When we think of "Star Wars: A New Hope," our minds immediately conjure images of iconic characters like Luke Skywalker, Princess Leia, and Han Solo, but what if I told you that the faces we associate with these roles almost looked entirely different? The casting choices for this groundbreaking film were as adventurous as the story itself, filled with unexpected turns and intriguing possibilities that could have altered the course of cinematic history.

Let's start with the central figure, Luke Skywalker. Originally, the role was offered to a number of actors before Mark Hamill landed it. Among those considered were actors like Al Pacino, who was at the peak of his career, and even Kurt Russell, who was making a name for himself in Hollywood. Imagine Pacino, with his intense gaze and dramatic flair, trying to embody the optimistic farm boy from Tatooine. It's a fascinating thought, but it's hard to picture him wielding a lightsaber, isn't it? The essence of Luke was that of an everyman, a character we could relate to, and Hamill's portrayal captured that youthful innocence and determination perfectly.

Then there's Princess Leia, a role that was almost played by a different actress entirely. The legendary actress and screenwriter, Carrie Fisher, ultimately made the character her own, but before her, names like Sissy Spacek and even Jodie Foster were in the running. Spacek, known for her nuanced performances, would have brought a different energy to Leia, perhaps a more fragile interpretation, while Foster's intelligence and strength could have created a more cerebral version of the character. Yet, it's Fisher's blend of sass and strength that resonated with audiences, making Leia a feminist icon long before the term was widely recognized.

And what about Han Solo? Harrison Ford's portrayal is so ingrained in our cultural consciousness that it's hard to imagine anyone else in the role. However, the casting process was extensive. Actors like Al Pacino were considered again, as was Burt Reynolds, who was known for his charm and charisma. But the most intriguing alternative was actually a young actor named Christopher Walken. Can you picture Walken's unique delivery and quirky charisma as the roguish smuggler? It's an intriguing thought, but Ford's combination of charisma, humor, and ruggedness created a character that is still celebrated in pop culture today.

The casting choices extended beyond the main trio as well. For Obi-Wan Kenobi, the role was initially offered to the esteemed British actor, Sir Alec Guinness. However, before Guinness accepted, other actors were considered, including the legendary Peter Cushing, who eventually portrayed the villainous Grand Moff Tarkin. Cushing's gravitas would have brought a different flavor to the wise Jedi Master, but Guinness's subtlety and depth allowed Obi-Wan to resonate with audiences in ways that were unexpected for a character who could have easily been a mere mentor figure.

Let's not forget the dark side. Darth Vader's voice was famously provided by James Earl Jones, but the physicality of the character was brought to life by David Prowse, a British bodybuilder. Initially, there was talk of casting a different actor for the voice, but Jones's deep, commanding presence became synonymous with the character. Imagine if someone else had voiced Vader; it could have changed the entire tone of the character, making him less imposing, less memorable.

In retrospect, the casting decisions for "Star Wars: A New Hope" were pivotal, not just for the film, but for the entire franchise and the landscape of science fiction cinema. Each actor brought their unique talents and interpretations, shaping the characters into the legends we know today. The film's success was a combination of vision, timing, and, of course, the right people in the right roles. It's a testament to how casting can make or break a film, and how the choices made in the early stages of production can echo throughout the decades, influencing generations of filmmakers and fans alike.

The Art of Casting: How Spielberg's Unconventional Choices Brought "Schindler's List" to Life

When we think about iconic films, especially those that tackle heavy historical themes, the casting choices often play a pivotal role in shaping the narrative and emotional weight of the story. "Schindler's List," directed by Steven Spielberg and released in 1993, is one such film that resonates deeply with audiences. However, the path to casting the right actors for this monumental project was anything but straightforward. Originally, Spielberg envisioned a different set of actors to portray the characters who would ultimately become etched in cinematic history.

Consider the lead role of Oskar Schindler. Initially, Spielberg had his sights set on a few major names, including Kevin Costner and Al Pacino. These actors were at the height of their careers and would have brought a different energy to the character. Costner, known for his roles in films like "Dances with Wolves," embodied a rugged charm, while Pacino, with his intense and often volatile performances, could have infused Schindler with a raw emotional edge. However, as Spielberg delved deeper into the story and the character's complexities, he began to lean towards a more unconventional choice: Liam Neeson. Neeson, who was still on the rise at the time, ultimately brought a nuanced depth to Schindler, capturing the transformation of a man who began as a war profiteer and evolved into a savior of over a thousand Jews during the Holocaust.

Then there was the character of Amon Goeth, the sadistic Nazi officer. Initially, Spielberg had considered casting the renowned actor and filmmaker, Roman Polanski, who had a personal connection to the Holocaust as a survivor. However, Polanski's involvement would have posed significant challenges, given his own tumultuous history and the complexities surrounding him. Instead, Ralph Fiennes stepped into the role, delivering a chilling performance that left an indelible mark on audiences. Fiennes embodied Goeth's chilling demeanor and moral depravity, and his portrayal became one of the most haunting aspects of the film. His ability to oscillate between moments of calm and explosive violence made the character terrifyingly real, and it's hard to imagine anyone else in that role after seeing his performance.

The casting of the supporting characters also underwent significant changes throughout the pre-production phase. Spielberg initially approached actors like John Malkovich and even Robert De Niro for various roles, but as the project progressed, the director sought authenticity. He decided to cast many Jewish actors, aligning with his vision of depicting the historical events with the utmost respect and accuracy. This decision not only added a layer of authenticity but also provided opportunities for lesser-known actors to shine. For example, Ben Kingsley, who played Itzhak Stern, Schindler's Jewish accountant, brought a gravitas to the role that was essential in portraying the moral dilemmas faced by those living in such dire circumstances.

Moreover, the decision to cast non-professional actors in certain roles, particularly in the concentration camp scenes, was a bold choice that added to the film's realism. Spielberg wanted to capture the raw emotions of the Holocaust, and by incorporating real people who had lived through such horrors, he created a visceral experience for the audience. This approach was not without its challenges, as many of these actors had never performed before, but their authenticity resonated powerfully on screen.

Ultimately, the casting choices for "Schindler's List" reflect a broader commitment to storytelling that prioritizes truth and emotional resonance over star power. Each actor, whether they were a household name or a newcomer, contributed to the film's profound impact. The decisions made during the casting process were not just about filling roles; they were about honoring history, evoking empathy, and ensuring that the voices of those who suffered were heard. In the end, the film stands as a testament to the power of casting in shaping the narrative and emotional landscape of cinema, reminding us that behind every great film lies a story of choices that have the potential to change the world.

The Fascinating Original Casting Choices for Quentin Tarantino's "Pulp Fiction"

When we think of "Pulp Fiction," we often picture the iconic performances of John Travolta, Uma Thurman, and Samuel L. Jackson, but what if I told you that the film could have looked entirely different? The original casting choices for Quentin Tarantino's groundbreaking 1994 film reveal a fascinating web of what-ifs that could have changed the course of cinematic history.

First, let's talk about the role of Vincent Vega, the hitman played by Travolta, whose portrayal revitalized his career. Initially, Tarantino had envisioned a different actor for this role, someone who could bring a certain edge and charisma to the character. Can you imagine the film with Michael Madsen in the lead? Madsen, who eventually played the role of Mr. Blonde in "Reservoir Dogs," was one of Tarantino's go-to actors. His rugged demeanor and tough-guy image would have certainly added a different flavor to the film. Madsen's take on Vincent could have leaned more toward the brooding and dangerous side, possibly altering the film's tone significantly.

Then there's the role of Jules Winnfield, the philosophical hitman with a penchant for quoting scripture. Samuel L. Jackson's portrayal is now iconic, but originally, Tarantino considered other actors as well. One of the names that surfaced was Laurence Fishburne. Fishburne, known for his powerful performances, could have brought a different intensity to Jules. Imagine him delivering those famous monologues about the "path of the righteous man" with his unique gravitas. It's intriguing to think about how his presence might have shifted the dynamics between the characters, perhaps making the film feel more serious and less playful in its violence.

The role of Mia Wallace, the enigmatic wife of mob boss Marsellus Wallace, was also subject to interesting casting choices. While Uma Thurman ultimately nailed the part, there were discussions about casting actresses like Meg Ryan or even Drew Barrymore. Ryan, with her girl-next-door charm, could have created a contrasting dynamic with Vincent, giving the character a more innocent vibe. On the other hand, Barrymore, who was initially cast for the role of the young woman in the opening scene, could have brought a different kind of energy to Mia, perhaps infusing the character with a more playful and whimsical quality. It's fascinating to ponder how these actresses might have interpreted Mia's mix of vulnerability and danger.

And let's not forget about the character of Butch Coolidge, the boxer played by Bruce Willis. Tarantino had originally considered actors like Matt Dillon and even Tom Cruise for this role. Dillon, known for his bad-boy persona, could have given Butch a different edge, while Cruise, with his undeniable charm, might have turned the character into a more likable figure, potentially altering the audience's perception of him throughout the film. The casting of Butch is crucial because it sets the tone for the entire narrative arc, and the choices here could have shifted the film's focus from a gritty crime drama to something more mainstream.

One cannot overlook the supporting roles, either. The character of Pumpkin, played by Tim Roth, was originally supposed to be portrayed by actors like Johnny Depp or even Steve Buscemi. Depp's quirky charm could have brought a different layer of humor to the character, while Buscemi, known for his unique style, might have infused Pumpkin with an eccentricity that would have been unforgettable.

In the end, the casting of "Pulp Fiction" was a perfect storm of talent, timing, and Tarantino's unique vision. The choices made not only shaped the film but also influenced the careers of those involved. Each actor brought their own flavor to the roles, creating a masterpiece that has stood the test of time. The original casting choices serve as a reminder of how different the film could have been, and how the right actor in the right role can create magic on screen.

How Barbra Streisand, Faye Dunaway and others missed out on "Cabaret"

When we think of the iconic film "Cabaret," our minds often drift to the unforgettable performances of Liza Minnelli as Sally Bowles and Joel Grey as the Master of Ceremonies. However, the journey to casting these roles was anything but straightforward. The original casting choices for this seminal film reveal a fascinating intersection of talent, vision, and circumstance that ultimately shaped the movie's legacy.

Initially, the role of Sally Bowles was offered to a range of established actresses, each bringing their own unique flair to the character. Among them was the legendary Barbra Streisand, who was riding high on the success of her Broadway career. Streisand's powerful voice and magnetic stage presence made her a prime candidate, but her commitment to other projects ultimately prevented her from taking on the role. Then there was the equally captivating Faye Dunaway, whose star was on the rise. Dunaway had a certain intensity that could have brought a different dimension to Sally, but she too was unable to commit, leaving the door open for others.

Interestingly, the filmmakers also considered several lesser-known actresses, tapping into a pool of emerging talent. One such name was Jill Haworth, who had already made her mark on Broadway in the original production of "Cabaret." Haworth's experience with the character gave her an edge, and she was ultimately cast in the stage version. However, when it came to the film adaptation, her name was overshadowed by the likes of Minnelli, who, at the time, was a rising star but not yet the household name she would become.

The role of the Emcee, played by Joel Grey, also had its share of casting drama. Originally, the filmmakers envisioned a more flamboyant figure, someone who could embody the wild spirit of the Weimar Republic. Names like Gene Wilder were floated around, and while Wilder was undoubtedly talented, his comedic style led the producers to reconsider their direction. They sought someone who could seamlessly blend humor with a darker, more sinister undertone. Grey, already an accomplished Broadway performer, stepped into the role with a unique blend of charm and menace that transformed the character into an unforgettable icon. His portrayal became a defining aspect of the film, cementing his place in cinematic history.

As the casting process unfolded, the tension between the original vision and the evolving landscape of Hollywood became increasingly apparent. The film was set against the backdrop of a tumultuous era, both politically and socially, and the casting choices reflected a desire to capture that complexity. The filmmakers were acutely aware that they needed actors who could not only perform but also resonate with the changing attitudes of the 1970s audience. This led to a more nuanced approach, one that ultimately favored Minnelli, whose ability to convey vulnerability and resilience made her the perfect choice for the role of Sally Bowles.

The chemistry between Minnelli and Grey added another layer to the film. Their performances were not just about individual talent; they were about creating a world where the characters could thrive. The original casting choices, while intriguing, ultimately led to a dynamic pairing that would become synonymous with "Cabaret." Their interpretations of the material injected new life into the story, allowing the film to transcend its stage origins.

In retrospect, the casting of "Cabaret" serves as a testament to the unpredictable nature of filmmaking. The choices made, the names considered, and the talent ultimately selected all contributed to a cultural phenomenon that has endured through the decades. The film's legacy is a reminder that sometimes, the path to greatness is paved with unexpected detours and the willingness to embrace the unknown. It's a narrative woven into the very fabric of cinema history, celebrating the serendipity of casting and the lasting impact of artistry.

The Actors Who Almost Became Batman: A Journey Through Hollywood's What-Ifs

In the realm of cinematic history, few characters have undergone as many transformations as Batman. The caped crusader, with his dark persona and complex psychology, has captivated audiences for decades. However, what many may not realize is that the journey to the silver screen was fraught with unexpected casting choices that could have altered the very fabric of the franchise. Let's take a closer look at those original casting choices that could have changed the face of Gotham forever.

When Tim Burton was brought on board to direct the 1989 Batman film, the landscape of superhero movies was vastly different from what we know today. The genre was still finding its footing, and the idea of a darker, more brooding Batman was a radical departure from the campy television series of the 1960s. Burton envisioned a darker tone, and with that vision came the need for a leading man who could embody the duality of Bruce Wayne and Batman.

Initially, the role was offered to several high-profile actors. One of the first names that emerged was Mel Gibson. At the time, Gibson was riding high on the success of the "Lethal Weapon" franchise, and his rugged charm and intensity made him a strong contender. However, Gibson ultimately passed on the role, perhaps sensing that the character required a depth that he was not ready to explore. His decision paved the way for other actors to step into the shadows.

Another surprising candidate was Bill Murray. Known primarily for his comedic roles, Murray's name was floated as a potential Batman. The idea of a comedic actor taking on such a serious role raised eyebrows. While Murray has proven his versatility over the years, the notion of him donning the cape and cowl feels almost absurd in retrospect. Can you imagine the wisecracks and deadpan humor interspersed with the dark narrative of Gotham? It would have been a film unlike any other, but perhaps not in the way anyone would have hoped.

Then there was the intriguing choice of Kevin Costner. Fresh off the success of "Dances with Wolves," Costner was a major box office draw. His rugged good looks and brooding presence seemed like a perfect fit for the role. However, Costner ultimately opted to pursue other projects, leaving the door open for someone else to take on the mantle. It's fascinating to consider how Costner's portrayal might have influenced the character's trajectory in subsequent films.

And who could forget the name of Charlie Sheen? At the time, he was a rising star, and the idea of him as Batman was floated around. Sheen, with his rebellious spirit and undeniable charisma, could have brought a different energy to the role. However, the notion of a young Sheen donning the cape feels like a missed opportunity that could have resulted in a very different interpretation of the character. Could Sheen have successfully balanced the duality of Bruce Wayne's charm and Batman's intensity? It's a tantalizing question.

Ultimately, the role of Batman went to Michael Keaton, a choice that surprised many. Keaton, known for his comedic performances in films like "Beetlejuice," was an unconventional pick. However, Burton saw something in him that resonated with the darker aspects of the character. Keaton's portrayal redefined Batman for a new generation, proving that the right actor could transcend preconceived notions and bring depth to the role.

As we look back at these original casting choices, it's clear that the path to Batman's cinematic legacy was paved with intriguing possibilities. Each actor brought their own unique flair, and while some may have seemed like outlandish choices, they reflect the ever-evolving nature of storytelling in Hollywood. The casting of Batman is a reminder that sometimes the most unexpected choices can lead to the most iconic portrayals. In the end, it was Michael Keaton who embraced the darkness, and in doing so, he set the stage for the enduring legacy of the Dark Knight.

The Alternate Supermen: The Surprising Actors Who Could Have Played the Man of Steel

When we think about the iconic film "Superman," released in 1978, it's hard not to envision Christopher Reeve in that unforgettable role. His portrayal of the Man of Steel became the gold standard for superhero films, but what many people might not realize is that the path to casting him was anything but straightforward. The journey of finding the right actor for Superman is a fascinating tale filled with twists, turns, and a surprising array of choices that could have changed the face of superhero cinema forever.

Initially, the filmmakers had a clear vision of what they wanted. They were looking for someone who could embody the duality of Clark Kent and Superman, someone who could convincingly portray both the mild-mannered reporter and the powerful alien hero. The casting team considered numerous actors before settling on Reeve. Among the early contenders was the legendary actor Al Pacino. Yes, the same man who would go on to define characters like Michael Corleone in "The Godfather." Pacino was a hot commodity in Hollywood, and his name was thrown around in discussions about the role. However, Pacino was more interested in other projects, and the idea of him donning the cape and tights ultimately faded away.

Another name that surfaced during the casting process was Robert Redford. At the time, Redford was one of the biggest stars in Hollywood, known for his charm and rugged good looks. Imagine the suave, charismatic Redford soaring through the skies of Metropolis.

While he would have undoubtedly brought a different energy to the role, he ultimately passed on the opportunity, feeling that the character was not a fit for him. The filmmakers continued their search, casting a wide net across Hollywood.

One of the more surprising choices was the actor Burt Reynolds. Reynolds was at the peak of his career, known for his roles in films like "Smokey and the Bandit" and "Deliverance." He had the charisma and physicality that could have made him a compelling Superman. However, Reynolds also had reservations about the role, believing that the character was too wholesome and did not align with his own image, which leaned more towards the rebellious and rugged. It's fascinating to think how a Reynolds-led Superman might have shifted the tone of the film entirely.

Then there were the lesser-known actors who were considered. Names like Jon Voight and even a young, up-and-coming actor named Arnold Schwarzenegger were in the mix. Voight, with his intense acting style, could have brought a different gravitas to the character, while Schwarzenegger, at that time, was still building his reputation in Hollywood. The thought of him in a spandex suit might seem ludicrous now, but it's a testament to the era's evolving view of what a superhero could be.

As the casting process continued, the filmmakers began to narrow their focus. They were looking for an actor who could not only act but also embody the physicality of Superman. This quest led them to the relatively unknown Christopher Reeve, who had recently appeared in a few films but had not yet achieved stardom. His audition was a revelation; he brought a blend of charm, sincerity, and strength that perfectly captured the essence of Superman. The moment he stepped into the role, everything clicked. It was as if he had been born to play the part.

Reeve's casting was a pivotal moment not just for the film but for the entire genre of superhero movies. His performance set a benchmark that influenced countless portrayals of superheroes in the years to come. The original casting choices for "Superman" remind us of the unpredictable nature of filmmaking. Each actor considered brought their unique flavor to the table, but in the end, it was Reeve who soared above the rest, forever etching his name in the annals of cinematic history. The story of casting "Superman" serves as a reminder that sometimes the most unexpected choices lead to the most legendary outcomes.

Casting a Different Spell: The Fascinating Story of Who Almost Played the Roles in 'The Lord of the Rings' Classic Trilogy

When we think of the iconic film trilogy, "The Lord of the Rings," directed by Peter Jackson, it's hard to imagine anyone else in those beloved roles. However, the original casting choices tell a fascinating story of what could have been. Let's dive into the casting decisions that shaped the journey to Middle-earth and how they could have altered the cinematic landscape we know today.

First, let's talk about Frodo Baggins, the heart of the story. Elijah Wood's portrayal has become synonymous with the character, but he wasn't the first choice. Initially, the role was offered to actors like Jake Gyllenhaal and even a young, fresh-faced Macaulay Culkin. Can you imagine Culkin, with his childlike charm, embarking on such a dark and perilous journey? It's intriguing to think about how different the emotional depth of Frodo would have felt in the hands of these actors. Gyllenhaal, with his intense performances, might have brought a different kind of gravitas to the role, but Wood's vulnerability ultimately captured Frodo's essence perfectly.

Then we have Aragorn, the rugged ranger destined to become king. Viggo Mortensen's portrayal is legendary, but he was not the first choice either. Initially, the role was offered to actors like Nicolas Cage and Russell Crowe. Cage, known for his eccentric performances, might have brought a unique flair to Aragorn, but would he have been able to convey the character's complexity? Crowe, on the other hand, could have infused Aragorn with a more aggressive edge, but Mortensen's nuanced performance, balancing strength and sensitivity, truly embodied the character's journey from ranger to king.

And what about the wise and powerful Gandalf? Ian McKellen's performance is iconic, but he wasn't the first actor considered for the role. The legendary Sean Connery was approached, and he famously turned it down. Imagine Connery's commanding presence as Gandalf! It's hard to picture anyone else delivering those profound lines with such gravitas. McKellen, however, brought a warmth and depth to the character that resonated with audiences, making Gandalf a beloved figure. It's a testament to how casting can shape a character's legacy.

Now, let's not forget about the hobbits. The casting of the Fellowship is crucial, and while Wood shone as Frodo, the original casting for Samwise Gamgee was a bit of a rollercoaster. Actors like Simon Pegg were considered, which would have brought a comedic twist to Sam's loyal and steadfast nature. Pegg's humor is undeniable, but would it have undercut the emotional weight of Sam's character? Ultimately, Sean Astin's portrayal brought a perfect blend of loyalty, bravery, and heart, grounding Frodo's journey in friendship.

The casting choices extended beyond the main characters. Consider Legolas, originally envisioned for actors like Orlando Bloom, who ultimately got the role, versus the likes of David Beckham, who was once in the running. Beckham's casting would have undoubtedly attracted a different audience, but could he have delivered the ethereal quality and agility that Bloom brought to the character? The same goes for Gimli, portrayed by John Rhys-Davies, who was initially not the first choice either. The chemistry and camaraderie he shared with the rest of the cast became a hallmark of the trilogy, showcasing how the right choices can create magic on screen.

As we reflect on these original casting choices, it becomes clear that while the final selections for "The Lord of the Rings" were spot on, the journey to those decisions was filled with intriguing possibilities. Each actor brought their own unique flair to the characters, and the chemistry among the cast ultimately shaped the story we know and love. The "what ifs" linger in the air, but they also highlight the importance of casting in bringing a story to life, reminding us that sometimes, the stars align just right to create something truly unforgettable.

Saving Private Ryan: The Alternate Realities of Casting

When we think of "Saving Private Ryan," we often focus on its visceral depiction of World War II, the harrowing battles, and the emotional weight of sacrifice. However, behind its monumental success lies a fascinating tale of casting that could have dramatically altered the film's trajectory. The original casting choices for Steven Spielberg's 1998 classic reveal a landscape of what-ifs that are both intriguing and insightful.

Initially, the role of Captain Miller, the stoic leader tasked with finding and bringing home Private James Ryan, was offered to several high-profile actors before Tom Hanks ultimately secured it. Among those considered were the likes of Mel Gibson and Harrison Ford. Each of these actors brought their unique charisma and star power to the table. Mel Gibson, known for his intense performances and action-hero persona, could have infused the character with a different kind of ruggedness, perhaps leaning more towards the archetypal warrior. On the other hand, Harrison Ford, with his iconic roles in "Star Wars" and "Indiana Jones," might have brought a sense of adventure and charm to Captain Miller, making him a leader with undeniable charisma. Yet, it was Hanks' ability to convey vulnerability and depth that ultimately resonated with Spielberg and the audience. His portrayal of a man burdened by the weight of command and the horrors of war became a defining aspect of the film.

Then there's the character of Private Ryan himself, originally envisioned to be played by a different actor. Before Matt Damon was cast, the role was reportedly offered to Edward Norton, who was fresh off the success of "Primal Fear." Norton, with his intense and often brooding performances, could have presented a different kind of Ryan—one perhaps more introspective and complex. However, casting Damon, who was just beginning to rise in Hollywood, added a sense of relatability and earnestness to the character. Damon's performance captured the essence of an ordinary man thrust into extraordinary circumstances, embodying the everyman that audiences could connect with.

Another interesting casting choice was that of Sergeant Horvath, a role that ultimately went to Tom Sizemore. Before Sizemore stepped into the boots of the grizzled sergeant, actors like John C. Reilly and even the late Philip Seymour Hoffman were in the mix. Reilly, known for his comedic chops, might have brought a lighter, more humorous touch to the character, contrasting the grim realities of war. Hoffman, on the other hand, could have infused the role with a profound sense of tragedy and depth, perhaps making Horvath a more tortured soul. Sizemore's portrayal, however, struck a balance between toughness and camaraderie, grounding the film in a gritty realism that resonated with audiences.

The casting choices didn't stop there. The role of Wade, the medic, was initially considered for several actors, including the talented Giovanni Ribisi, who eventually did land the role. However, before him, there were discussions about casting someone like Billy Crudup, who would have brought a different energy to the character. Ribisi's performance, with its mix of vulnerability and determination, became a poignant reminder of the fragility of life amidst the chaos of war.

As we delve into these casting choices, it's clear that "Saving Private Ryan" was a film shaped not only by its script and direction but also by the actors who brought these characters to life. Each potential casting decision offers a glimpse into alternate realities where the film could have taken on entirely different tones and messages. The chemistry between the cast members, the emotional arcs of their characters, and the overall impact of the film were all influenced by these choices.

In the end, while we may never know how the film would have turned out with a different ensemble, the final casting decisions contributed to a powerful narrative that remains etched in cinematic history. "Saving Private Ryan" stands as a testament to the art of filmmaking, where every choice, down to the actors, plays a crucial role in shaping the story we ultimately experience.

Reckless Ambition: The Surprising Casting Choices Behind the Wolf of Wall Street

When we talk about "The Wolf of Wall Street," directed by Martin Scorsese and based on Jordan Belfort's memoir, we often focus on the performances of Leonardo DiCaprio, Jonah Hill, and Margot Robbie. However, the casting process for this film was a fascinating journey filled with unexpected twists and turns, revealing how the right actors can transform a narrative. Initially, DiCaprio was always in the conversation for the role of Belfort. His connection to the project dates back to 2007 when he first expressed interest in the story. But it wasn't a straightforward path. At one point, the role of Belfort was considered for other actors as well. Names like Brad Pitt and even Christian Bale floated around, both of whom brought their unique styles and gravitas to the table. Imagine a version of this film with Pitt's charismatic charm or Bale's intense commitment to character. The dynamics would have shifted dramatically, and perhaps the portrayal of the infamous stockbroker would have taken on a different flavor.

Jonah Hill, who eventually stepped into the role of Donnie Azoff, was not the first choice either. Initially, the filmmakers looked at a variety of actors, including the likes of James Franco and Seth Rogen. Each of these actors would have brought their comedic styles to the role, but Hill's ability to blend humor with a more serious undertone made him the perfect fit. His chemistry with DiCaprio is palpable, creating a partnership that truly drives the film. Hill's audition process was particularly interesting; he had to demonstrate not just his comedic chops but also his ability to embody the reckless abandon that characterized Azoff's life. It was a risk, but one that paid off handsomely.

Then there's Margot Robbie, who delivered a breakout performance as Naomi Lapaglia. Initially, the filmmakers considered a range of actresses, including some big names from the industry who could have brought their own interpretations to the role. However, Robbie's audition was a game-changer. She brought a fierce energy and a captivating presence that made her stand out from the rest. The chemistry between her and DiCaprio was immediate, and it was clear that she could hold her own against him, a critical factor in a film that hinges on the dynamic between its two leads.

The casting of "The Wolf of Wall Street" was not just about finding recognizable faces; it was about assembling a group of actors who could authentically portray the excess and moral ambiguity of the characters they were playing. The original casting choices reveal a lot about the film's potential direction. For instance, if the role of Belfort had gone to a different actor, the tone might have shifted dramatically. The film is as much about the wild, frenetic energy of Wall Street in the 1990s as it is about the characters' moral decay.

Additionally, the casting process was influenced by the script's evolution. Scorsese and his team were not just looking for actors; they were searching for collaborators who could contribute to the film's overall vision. This is why some actors who were initially considered ultimately didn't fit the final vision, even if they were talented.

In the end, the casting choices made for "The Wolf of Wall Street" were not just about star power; they were about finding the right fit for a narrative that demanded authenticity, charisma, and a certain level of recklessness. The actors who ultimately took on these roles brought a unique energy that transformed the film into the cultural phenomenon it became. It's a reminder of how crucial casting is in filmmaking, shaping not just the characters but the very essence of the story being told. The journey of casting this film is a testament to the idea that sometimes, the best choices are the ones that surprise us the most.

"Platoon" Revisited: The Fascinating Journey to the Final Cast of Oliver Stone's War Movie

When we think about the film "Platoon," directed by Oliver Stone and released in 1986, we often envision the intense performances of its cast, the visceral depiction of the Vietnam War, and the haunting moral dilemmas faced by soldiers. However, the journey to the final cast was filled with intriguing choices and near-misses that could have dramatically altered the film's legacy. The original casting choices for "Platoon" reveal a fascinating landscape of Hollywood dynamics, personal ambitions, and the unpredictable nature of the film industry.

Oliver Stone, a Vietnam veteran himself, wanted to create a film that was as authentic as possible, reflecting his own experiences in the war. He envisioned a cast that could embody the complexity and turmoil of soldiers in combat. Initially, the role of Chris Taylor, the film's protagonist, was offered to several actors who were prominent at the time. Tom Cruise was one of the first choices. Imagine Cruise, with his boyish charm and intensity, attempting to portray a soldier grappling with the moral ambiguities of war. However, Cruise was unable to commit due to scheduling conflicts with "Top Gun," which ultimately paved the way for Charlie Sheen to step into the role. Sheen's performance brought a raw vulnerability that resonated deeply with audiences, but it's intriguing to consider how Cruise's star power might have shifted the film's reception.

Another notable casting consideration was for the character of Sergeant Elias, a role that ultimately went to Willem Dafoe. Initially, Stone had his eye on a different actor, one who would bring a unique intensity to the character. The legendary actor Al Pacino was approached for the role. Pacino, known for his electrifying performances in films like "The Godfather" and "Scarface," could have brought a different energy to Elias, one that might have intensified the character's moral struggle. However, Pacino was not interested in the role, feeling it was too similar to the characters he had portrayed in the past. Dafoe's eventual casting not only brought the character to life with a haunting depth but also became a defining moment in his career, showcasing his ability to embody complex, conflicted characters.

Then there was the role of Barnes, the brutal and hardened sergeant, originally intended for another heavyweight actor, originally considered was Robert De Niro. De Niro, fresh off his iconic role in "Raging Bull," was a natural choice for a character who embodies the darker side of military leadership. However, De Niro declined the role, and Stone turned to Tom Berenger, who ultimately delivered a chilling performance that perfectly captured Barnes' ruthless nature. Berenger's portrayal added layers to the character, making him both a terrifying figure and a tragic one, a complexity that might have been different with De Niro's interpretation.

The casting of the supporting roles also tells its own story. The character of King, a soldier who becomes emblematic of the war's senselessness, was originally considered for actor Sean Penn. Penn, who was emerging as a powerful force in Hollywood, could have brought a different perspective to the character. However, scheduling conflicts with other projects prevented him from taking the role, allowing for the talented Keith David to step in and leave his mark on the film.

As we reflect on the original casting choices for "Platoon," it becomes clear that the film's legacy could have taken many different paths. Each actor considered for these roles carried their own unique flair and interpretation, which could have shifted the film's impact significantly. The choices made ultimately shaped a narrative that resonated with audiences and critics alike, creating a powerful depiction of the Vietnam War that continues to be studied and revered today. In the end, the casting process for "Platoon" serves as a reminder of the delicate balance between vision and execution in filmmaking, where every choice can lead to a story that is both personal and universal.

The Roles That Could Have Been: Behind the Scenes of The Silence of the Lambs

When we think of iconic films, certain titles immediately come to mind, and "Silence of the Lambs" is undeniably one of them. Released in 1991, it has left an indelible mark on the landscape of cinema, particularly in the psychological thriller genre. But what many might not realize is that the casting choices for this film could have led to an entirely different experience. The path to casting the unforgettable characters of Dr. Hannibal Lecter and Clarice Starling was fraught with interesting twists and turns, revealing a fascinating behind-the-scenes story that adds layers to our understanding of this cinematic masterpiece.

Let's start with the character of Dr. Hannibal Lecter, a role that would ultimately be immortalized by Anthony Hopkins. However, Hopkins was not the first choice. In fact, the role was initially offered to the legendary actor Gene Hackman. Hackman, known for his remarkable versatility and depth, would have undoubtedly brought a unique interpretation to the character. Imagine the chilling, yet charismatic, presence he could have brought to the screen. However, Hackman turned down the role, feeling it was not the right fit for him. The casting team then considered other prominent actors, including Sean Connery and Al Pacino. Both actors had their own illustrious careers and could have delivered a powerful performance. However, for various reasons, they too passed on the opportunity.

Then came the moment when Anthony Hopkins entered the picture. His audition was a revelation. He brought a terrifying calmness to the character, a blend of sophistication and menace that was unlike anything seen before. His portrayal would eventually earn him an Academy Award for Best Actor, but it was his unique approach that truly set him apart. Hopkins famously studied the character of Lecter in depth, finding inspiration in the nuances of his speech and mannerisms. The result was a performance that not only defined the character but also redefined the horror genre itself.

Now, let's turn our attention to Clarice Starling, the determined FBI trainee played by Jodie Foster. Initially, the role was offered to several actresses, including Michelle Pfeiffer and Meg Ryan. Both were at the height of their careers and brought their own star power to the table. However, it was Jodie Foster, who had previously won an Oscar for her role in "The Accused," who ultimately embodied the character with a depth and complexity that resonated with audiences. Foster's portrayal was not just about being a strong female lead; it was about vulnerability and strength coexisting in a character who was navigating a male-dominated world.

Interestingly, the chemistry between Foster and Hopkins was not something that was guaranteed. Their dynamic was built on mutual respect and an understanding of their characters' psychological interplay. The tension and intrigue that unfolded on screen were a testament to their respective talents, but it was also a product of the casting process that had carefully selected actors who could bring these roles to life in a way that felt authentic and compelling.

The film's director, Jonathan Demme, played a crucial role in shaping the performances. He encouraged improvisation and allowed the actors to explore their characters' complexities. This approach not only enhanced the authenticity of the film but also created an atmosphere where Hopkins and Foster could thrive.

In retrospect, it's fascinating to consider how different "Silence of the Lambs" might have been had Gene Hackman, Sean Connery, or Michelle Pfeiffer taken on these pivotal roles. The film became a cultural phenomenon, not just because of its gripping narrative but also due to the haunting performances of its leads. The casting choices, which may have seemed like mere decisions at the time, ultimately shaped the film into the iconic work of art it is today. The legacy of "Silence of the Lambs" endures, in part, because of the serendipitous path that led to the perfect casting of two unforgettable characters.

How Different Casting Choices Could Have Changed the Course of "Chicago"

When we think of the movie "Chicago," we often envision the dazzling performances of Renée Zellweger, Catherine Zeta-Jones, and Richard Gere. However, the journey to the film's final casting was a winding road filled with intriguing choices and missed opportunities. The original casting decisions reveal a fascinating layer of Hollywood history that adds depth to our understanding of this iconic musical.

Initially, the role of Roxie Hart was considered for several high-profile actresses. Among them was the talented Drew Barrymore, who, at the time, was attempting to revitalize her career after a tumultuous period in the spotlight. Barrymore's name floated around as a potential Roxie, but as the project evolved, her involvement faded. The producers sought a more established star, and that's when Renée Zellweger entered the picture. Zellweger had gained recognition for her performances in films like "Bridget Jones's Diary," but taking on Roxie was a significant leap. She had to prove her mettle not just as an actress but also as a singer and dancer, which was a daunting challenge.

Then we have the role of Velma Kelly, originally considered for the sultry and charismatic Madonna. At the time, Madonna was at the peak of her popularity and had a strong connection to musical theater, having starred in "Evita." However, the producers were concerned about her acting abilities and the potential distraction her celebrity status could bring to the film. As the project progressed, they shifted their focus towards Catherine Zeta-Jones, who had just come off a string of successful films and was eager to showcase her musical talents. Zeta-Jones ultimately brought a fierce energy and sophistication to Velma that resonated with both audiences and critics alike.

Interestingly, the role of Billy Flynn, the slick lawyer, was initially envisioned for the legendary actor John Travolta. Travolta had a strong association with musicals thanks to his role in "Grease," and the producers believed he could bring a charismatic flair to the character. However, as discussions continued, Travolta's availability became a concern, and he ultimately passed on the project. This led the casting team to Richard Gere, who was an unexpected but brilliant choice. Gere infused Billy Flynn with a charm and wit that perfectly matched the character's manipulative nature, elevating the film's dynamic.

Another interesting casting tidbit involves the character of Mary Sunshine, the flamboyant reporter. The role was initially offered to the talented actress and singer, Liza Minnelli. Imagine the impact Minnelli could have had, given her status as a Broadway icon! However, scheduling conflicts and her commitment to other projects prevented her from taking on the role. Instead, the filmmakers cast Christine Baranski, whose sharp wit and vocal prowess brought a unique twist to Mary Sunshine, making her a memorable part of the ensemble.

As the casting process unfolded, the film's creative team faced the challenge of finding actors who could not only embody their characters but also bring the musical's vibrant spirit to life. The project was in development for years, and during that time, the landscape of Hollywood shifted. New stars emerged, and others faded, which influenced the final casting decisions. The film's eventual success can be attributed not only to the talent of its leading actors but also to the serendipitous nature of casting.

In the end, the original choices for "Chicago" paint a picture of a film that could have looked entirely different. Each actor brought their unique flair to the roles, but the initial casting considerations remind us of how close we came to a different interpretation of this classic story. The journey of "Chicago," from its stage origins to the screen, is a testament to the unpredictable nature of filmmaking and the magic that happens when the right actors come together to create something extraordinary.

From Pryor to Little: The Unlikely Evolution of 'Blazing Saddles'

When we think of "Blazing Saddles," we often envision the iconic performances of Cleavon Little as Bart and Gene Wilder as Jim, but the journey to the final casting was a winding road filled with unexpected choices and near-misses that could have changed the film entirely. The original casting choices were a reflection of the era's comedic landscape, and it's fascinating to consider how different the film might have been had those early decisions been finalized.

Initially, the role of Bart was offered to Richard Pryor, a groundbreaking comedian whose sharp wit and fearless approach to race and society would have added a unique flavor to the character. Pryor was not only a comedic genius but also someone who understood the complexities of race relations in America. However, due to various circumstances, including his struggles with substance abuse and a desire to remain behind the scenes, he ultimately declined the role. This decision opened the door for Cleavon Little, who brought his own charisma and depth to the character, creating a performance that would resonate with audiences for generations.

Interestingly, Pryor didn't just walk away from the project; he remained involved as a screenwriter. His collaboration with Mel Brooks and Andrew Bergman helped shape the script, infusing it with the edgy humor that became a hallmark of the film. Imagine Pryor's delivery in the lead role—his ability to blend humor with poignant social commentary could have transformed Bart into a character that was not only funny but also deeply reflective of the racial tensions of the time. This alternative vision is a tantalizing "what if" scenario that still sparks conversation among film enthusiasts today.

Another notable casting choice was the role of Jim, the Waco Kid. Initially, the filmmakers considered casting actors like Jack Lemmon or even the legendary John Wayne. Jack Lemmon, known for his comedic chops and versatility, would have brought a different energy to the film, perhaps leaning more into the traditional buddy-comedy dynamic. On the other hand, the idea of John Wayne, a symbol of rugged masculinity in Westerns, stepping into a comedic role like Jim is almost surreal. Wayne's involvement might have shifted the tone of the film dramatically, as his presence would have carried the weight of his iconic status, potentially overshadowing the satire that Brooks aimed to achieve.

Ultimately, Gene Wilder stepped into the role of Jim, and his chemistry with Cleavon Little became one of the film's most celebrated aspects. Wilder's ability to oscillate between deadpan humor and wild emotional outbursts created a dynamic that complemented Little's performance perfectly. The duo's banter and camaraderie not only provided comedic relief but also served to highlight the absurdity of the racial and social issues the film was tackling.

The casting of the supporting characters was equally intriguing. For instance, the role of the villainous Taggart was originally intended for other actors, but it was ultimately played by Slim Pickens, whose unique style brought an unexpected layer of humor to the character. Pickens' portrayal of a bumbling antagonist added to the film's satirical edge, making the absurdity of the Western genre even more pronounced.

As we look back at the original casting choices for "Blazing Saddles," it becomes clear that the film's legacy is not just a product of its script and direction but also of the remarkable talent that brought it to life. Each choice, from the leads to the supporting cast, contributed to a film that defied conventions and pushed boundaries. The alternate realities of casting decisions remind us that the magic of cinema often lies in the unexpected paths not taken. The film stands as a testament to the power of collaboration and the serendipity of casting, where the right actors at the right moment can turn a good script into a timeless classic.

When Wizardry Meets Reality: The Fascinating Casting Decisions Behind Harry Potter

When we think of the iconic characters from the Harry Potter series, it's almost impossible to separate them from the actors who brought them to life. However, the journey to casting these beloved roles was filled with intriguing choices and what-ifs that could have drastically altered the landscape of the Wizarding World as we know it. Let's take a moment to explore the original casting choices for the film adaptations of J.K. Rowling's magical saga, a journey that reveals the complexities of bringing such a beloved series to the big screen.

First, let's talk about Harry Potter himself. The role of the Boy Who Lived was ultimately played by Daniel Radcliffe, but the casting directors initially had a different vision. Before Radcliffe was even considered, the filmmakers looked at a myriad of young actors, including the likes of Tom Felton, who eventually landed the role of Draco Malfoy. Interestingly, the casting team even considered a young actor named Liam Aiken, who was known for his role in "Road to Perdition." Imagine if Aiken had donned the glasses and lightning bolt scar—his performance might have brought a different shade to Harry's character.

Then there's Hermione Granger. Emma Watson became synonymous with the role, but she wasn't the only one in the running. In fact, the casting team auditioned over 1,000 girls for Hermione. One notable contender was the young actress named Anna Chlumsky, who had made waves in the film "My Girl." Chlumsky's audition was impressive, but ultimately, the role went to Watson, whose portrayal brought Hermione's intelligence and bravery to life. It's fascinating to think of how different the dynamic of the trio could have been with a different actress in that role.

Now, let's not forget about Ron Weasley. The role was eventually filled by Rupert Grint, who had a unique audition that involved him performing a rap. However, before Grint was cast, there were whispers of other potential Rons. One name that often comes up is that of a young actor named Thomas Sangster, who later became known for his roles in "Love Actually" and "The Maze Runner." Sangster's charm and comedic timing could have offered a different flavor to Ron, but Grint's portrayal became a defining aspect of the series, bringing warmth and loyalty to the character.

As we delve deeper into the casting choices, we can't overlook the adult characters, particularly Albus Dumbledore. The late Richard Harris was the first to embody the role, bringing a gentle wisdom to the character. However, before Harris was cast, the filmmakers considered the legendary actor Ian McKellen. McKellen, who would later find fame as Gandalf in "The Lord of the Rings," had the gravitas to portray Dumbledore, and his involvement might have created a fascinating crossover of wizardly roles in fantasy cinema.

Similarly, the role of Severus Snape was eventually filled by Alan Rickman, whose portrayal became iconic. However, the casting team had originally considered other actors, including Tim Roth and even the renowned actor Hugo Weaving. Can you imagine a world where Snape's character was portrayed with a different intensity? The depth that Rickman brought to the role became a cornerstone of the series, but it's intriguing to ponder how the character's complexity might have shifted under different hands.

Through all these casting choices and near-misses, the Harry Potter films emerged as a cultural phenomenon, largely due to the chemistry and talent of the actors who were ultimately chosen. Each character, from the trio of Harry, Hermione, and Ron to the myriad of supporting roles, contributed to a tapestry that captivated audiences worldwide. While the original casting choices may have led us down alternate paths, the final selections became a testament to the magic of storytelling and the serendipity of casting. The world of Harry Potter is a reminder that sometimes the perfect fit is found in the most unexpected places, and the legacy of these characters will continue to enchant generations to come.

A Different Bonnie and Clyde: The What-If's of Hollywood's Casting Decisions

When we think of the iconic film "Bonnie and Clyde," released in 1967, we often picture the electric chemistry between Warren Beatty and Faye Dunaway, the two actors who ultimately brought the infamous outlaw couple to life. However, the casting process for this groundbreaking film was anything but straightforward, and the original choices for the roles reveal a fascinating glimpse into Hollywood's landscape during the 1960s.

Initially, the film was intended to be a project for the legendary director Arthur Penn, who had a vision for a gritty, realistic portrayal of the notorious criminals that captivated America during the Great Depression. Early on, Penn had his sights set on a different pair of actors to embody Bonnie Parker and Clyde Barrow. The first choice for Bonnie was actually the talented actress Anne Bancroft, who had already made a name for herself with her powerful performances in films such as "The Graduate." Bancroft's ability to convey both vulnerability and strength made her an intriguing option for the role of Bonnie, a character who was both fiercely independent and tragically flawed.

On the other hand, the role of Clyde was originally offered to the charismatic actor Jack Nicholson. At that time, Nicholson was beginning to make waves in Hollywood, known for his intense performances and a certain rebellious charm that made him a perfect fit for the role of a bank-robbing outlaw. The combination of Bancroft and

Nicholson seemed promising, hinting at a darker, edgier interpretation of Bonnie and Clyde that might have leaned more heavily into the psychological complexities of their characters.

However, as the project evolved, so did the casting. Arthur Penn and the producers began to reconsider their initial choices. They wanted a fresh dynamic, a pair that could capture the youthful exuberance and reckless abandon that defined the real-life Bonnie and Clyde. Enter Warren Beatty, who not only showed interest in the role of Clyde but also took on the responsibility of producing the film. Beatty's star power and his ability to embody the charm and danger of Clyde Barrow made him a natural fit, and his involvement brought a new level of excitement to the project.

As for Bonnie, the search continued until Faye Dunaway emerged as a frontrunner. Dunaway, who had already garnered critical acclaim for her work in films like "The Thomas Crown Affair," brought a unique blend of beauty and intensity to the role. The chemistry between Beatty and Dunaway was palpable, and their performances would ultimately redefine the way audiences viewed the outlaw couple.

Interestingly, the casting decisions were not solely based on acting ability. The film was released during a time of significant cultural upheaval in America, and the choice of actors reflected the shifting attitudes of the era. Beatty and Dunaway represented a new generation of Hollywood stars, embodying the youthful rebellion that resonated with audiences disillusioned by traditional values. Their portrayal of Bonnie and Clyde not only captured the romanticized allure of crime but also highlighted the tragic consequences of their choices, making the film a poignant commentary on the American experience.

Moreover, the casting process reveals the complexities of Hollywood's decision-making. The initial choices of Bancroft and Nicholson might have led to a completely different interpretation of the story, one that could have emphasized the darker psychological elements over the romanticized narrative that ultimately unfolded. The chemistry that Beatty and Dunaway shared was electric, and their performances became iconic, cementing them in cinematic history.

In retrospect, the journey of casting "Bonnie and Clyde" is a testament to the unpredictable nature of filmmaking. It shows how a project can evolve and change direction, often leading to unexpected and remarkable outcomes. The final result, with Beatty and Dunaway at the helm, not only captured the essence of Bonnie and Clyde but also left an indelible mark on American cinema, influencing countless films and actors in the years to come.

Hollywood's Original Plans for "The Poseidon Adventure" Were Dramatically Different

The Poseidon Adventure, a film that has become synonymous with disaster cinema, had a journey to its final casting that is as tumultuous as the plot itself. When we think of this iconic movie, we often picture the unforgettable performances of its lead actors. However, the original casting choices tell a fascinating story of what might have been, revealing the behind-the-scenes negotiations and the shifting landscape of Hollywood in the early 1970s.

Initially, the role of Captain Mike Rogo, portrayed by Ernest Borgnine, was intended for the legendary actor, John Wayne. Imagine the Duke, with his rugged charm and commanding presence, at the helm of a sinking ship. The producers envisioned Wayne as the embodiment of strength and resilience, but ultimately, his commitment to other projects and a desire to steer clear of a disaster film led to his withdrawal. This left the door open for Borgnine, who brought a different kind of depth to the character, blending vulnerability with authority, a choice that resonated deeply with audiences.

Then there was the role of the heroic and determined protagonist, Reverend Scott, originally eyed for the charismatic Frank Sinatra. Sinatra was a powerhouse in the entertainment industry, known for his magnetic performances and ability to draw in audiences. But as the project developed, it became clear that Sinatra's vision for the character diverged from what the filmmakers had in mind. His desire to inject a personal narrative into the role clashed with the ensemble-driven approach the creators were aiming for. This led to the casting of Gene Hackman, whose portrayal of Reverend Scott became a defining performance, showcasing a man of faith grappling with the chaos around him.

The character of Nonnie Parry, the young singer, was initially intended for the talented actress and singer, Barbra Streisand. Streisand was at the height of her fame, and the producers believed her star power would draw in audiences. However, she declined the role, feeling it was not substantial enough. This opened the door for the equally talented Carol Lynley, whose portrayal brought a sense of innocence and vulnerability to the character, adding a poignant layer to the film's emotional landscape.

Another intriguing casting choice was for the role of the wealthy, self-absorbed passenger, Belle Rosen. Originally, the part was offered to the incomparable Bette Davis. Davis, known for her fierce performances and larger-than-life persona, seemed a perfect fit for a character that would ultimately be a significant part of the ensemble. However, Davis's health issues and her reluctance to take on a supporting role led to the casting of Shelley Winters. Winters infused Belle with a mix of strength and fragility, culminating in a performance that not only garnered her an Academy Award nomination but also solidified her status as a leading lady in disaster films.

The character of the young couple, the Rosenbergs, was initially considered for a different pairing. The studio had approached the talented duo of Robert Redford and Mia Farrow, envisioning a youthful and dynamic representation of love amidst chaos. However, scheduling conflicts and creative differences led to the casting of Jack Albertson and Red Buttons, who brought a unique charm and humor to the film, making their characters memorable in their own right.

The Poseidon Adventure ultimately became a cultural phenomenon, but its original casting choices reflect a rich tapestry of Hollywood's evolution during the 1970s. Each actor who stepped into the roles brought their unique flair, transforming the film into a classic that continues to resonate with audiences today. The journey from initial casting to final performances reveals not just the fickle nature of Hollywood but also the serendipity that can occur when one door closes and another opens. The film stands as a testament to the idea that sometimes, the choices we make lead us to unexpected and extraordinary places, forever altering the course of storytelling in cinema.

The Unlikely Heroes: How "The Magnificent Seven" Came to Be

When we think of classic Westerns, few films stand out as prominently as "The Magnificent Seven." Released in 1960 and directed by John Sturges, this film is a reimagining of Akira Kurosawa's "Seven Samurai." It's a tale of courage, camaraderie, and the battle between good and evil. However, what's often overlooked is the fascinating journey of its casting, which almost reshaped the film into something entirely different.

Initially, the role of Chris Adams, the leader of the seven gunfighters, was envisioned for none other than the legendary actor, Steve McQueen. McQueen, with his rugged charisma and undeniable screen presence, seemed like a perfect fit for the role. However, in an interesting twist, he wasn't the first choice. The producers originally approached the iconic actor, Yul Brynner, who ultimately took on the role. Brynner, known for his commanding performances, brought a unique intensity to Chris Adams that would define the character. But it's intriguing to ponder what McQueen's interpretation might have looked like, given his own unique style and persona.

Then there's the character of Vin Tanner, originally intended for James Coburn. Coburn was an actor on the rise, known for his cool demeanor and sharp wit. However, due to scheduling conflicts, he was unable to take on the role. This led to another interesting casting decision: the role eventually went to Steve McQueen himself. This twist of fate not only allowed McQueen to shine but also highlighted the chemistry between him and Brynner, which became one of the film's most memorable aspects.

As the story unfolded, the search for the remaining five gunfighters revealed a plethora of intriguing casting choices. One of the most notable was the character of Lee, who was initially intended for actor Robert Vaughn. Vaughn was a talented performer, but his casting was not without controversy. The producers had considered several other actors, including the likes of Charlton Heston and even Frank Sinatra. Can you imagine Sinatra, with his suave demeanor, stepping into a role meant for a gritty gunslinger? It's a testament to the shifting landscape of Hollywood during that era, where the right fit could often come down to the smallest of details.

Another character, Harry Luck, was originally thought to be played by actor Eli Wallach. Wallach, known for his roles in various Westerns, would have brought a different flavor to the ensemble. Instead, the role went to the brilliant actor Brad Dexter, who infused Harry with a sense of humor and charm that resonated well with audiences. The chemistry among the cast was crucial, and the decisions made in casting created a dynamic that would ultimately elevate the film.

The character of Chico, the young and eager gunslinger, was initially offered to actor Tony Franciosa. However, Franciosa turned it down, leading to the casting of Horst Buchholz. Buchholz's portrayal added a youthful exuberance that contrasted beautifully with the more seasoned characters. This decision underscored the film's theme of mentorship and the passing of the torch, as the older gunfighters took the younger Chico under their wings.

As we delve deeper into the casting choices, it becomes evident that "The Magnificent Seven" was not just a product of its script or direction but a culmination of a series of serendipitous decisions. Each actor brought their own unique flair, creating a tapestry of personalities that made the film resonate with audiences. The original casting considerations reflect the shifting tides of Hollywood and the unpredictable nature of filmmaking.

Ultimately, the choices made in casting "The Magnificent Seven" set the stage for a film that would become a cornerstone of the Western genre. It's a reminder that sometimes, the path to greatness is paved with unexpected turns, and the legacy of those choices continues to influence filmmakers and actors to this day. The film remains a testament to the power of collaboration and the magic that can happen when the right people come together, even if it wasn't the original vision.

When Belushi Failed to Materialize: The Story of Ghostbusters' Original Casting

When we think of "Ghostbusters," the iconic 1984 film, we often picture the beloved ensemble of Bill Murray, Dan Aykroyd, Harold Ramis, and Ernie Hudson, but what if I told you that the original casting choices were quite different? The development of this film was a fascinating journey, marked by a series of intriguing decisions that would ultimately shape the landscape of comedy and cinema. The original concept for "Ghostbusters" began with Dan Aykroyd, who was inspired by his fascination with the paranormal and his love for science fiction. Aykroyd envisioned a film that combined elements of horror, comedy, and science fiction, and he initially wrote a script that featured characters who were not just ghost hunters but also interdimensional travelers.

In Aykroyd's original vision, the film was supposed to feature a much larger cast, including the likes of John Belushi, who was Aykroyd's close friend and collaborator. Belushi was initially slated to play the role of Peter Venkman, the wisecracking ghostbuster that Bill Murray would eventually embody. The chemistry between Aykroyd and Belushi was undeniable, and their previous work together on "The Blues Brothers" had set a precedent for their comedic partnership. However, tragedy struck when Belushi passed away in 1982, leaving a significant void in the project. This loss forced Aykroyd and the producers to rethink their casting strategy.

As they searched for a replacement for Belushi, they considered several other prominent comedians of the time. Chevy Chase was one of the first names that came up. His background in sketch comedy and his experience on "Saturday Night Live" made him a prime candidate. However, scheduling conflicts with other projects ultimately led to his decline of the role. The filmmakers then turned their attention to a lesser-known actor who had been making waves in the comedy scene: Bill Murray. Murray's deadpan delivery and unique comedic style brought a fresh energy to the character, leading to the iconic portrayal we know today.

As the casting process continued, the role of Egon Spengler, originally envisioned as a more eccentric character, was intended for the likes of either Christopher Walken or even the legendary comedian, Steve Martin. However, the producers ultimately settled on Harold Ramis, who not only brought his comedic talent but also infused the character with an intellectual charm that was pivotal to the film's dynamic. Ramis, who co-wrote the screenplay, understood the balance between comedy and the supernatural that Aykroyd had envisioned, making him an integral part of the film's success.

Then there's Winston Zeddemore, a character who was not in Aykroyd's original draft. The role was created to add diversity to the cast and to bring in a character who was more grounded and relatable to the audience. Initially, Eddie Murphy was considered for this role, and the idea of him as a ghostbuster is tantalizing. His comedic prowess was undeniable, and he would have brought a different flair to the group. However, Murphy was also tied up with other commitments, leading to the eventual casting of Ernie Hudson. Hudson's portrayal of Winston provided the film with a sense of normalcy amid the chaos, and his character's everyman perspective resonated with audiences.

The casting of "Ghostbusters" was not simply a matter of finding the right actors; it was a complex web of timing, chemistry, and the tragic loss of a comedic icon. Each decision made during the casting process contributed to the film's legacy, which has endured for decades. The combination of Aykroyd's vision, Murray's improvisational genius,

Ramis's intellect, and Hudson's groundedness created a perfect storm of talent that not only made "Ghostbusters" a box office success but also a cultural phenomenon. It's a testament to how the right casting choices can transform a script into something truly magical, echoing through the annals of film history.

A Closer Look at The Phantom of the Opera's Casting Choices:

When we think of "The Phantom of the Opera," the mind often drifts to the haunting melodies, the elaborate sets, and, of course, the iconic characters that have captivated audiences for decades. However, before the film graced the silver screen, there was a fascinating journey of casting that almost altered the very fabric of this beloved story. The original casting choices for the movie reveal a tapestry of ambition, talent, and sometimes, sheer serendipity.

To start with, let's consider the character of the Phantom himself. The role demands a unique blend of charisma, mystery, and a touch of darkness. Initially, the filmmakers had their sights set on a variety of actors who could embody the tortured genius of Erik, the Phantom. Names like Antonio Banderas and even the legendary Michael Crawford, who had famously portrayed the Phantom in the original stage production, floated around. Imagine Banderas, with his smoldering intensity, bringing a different kind of passion to the role, or Crawford, who had already defined the character for a generation, stepping back into the shadows of the opera house. But ultimately, the role was given to Gerard Butler, whose own interpretation brought a raw and rugged edge that resonated with audiences, albeit not without its share of criticism.

Then, there's Christine Daaé, the ethereal soprano who captures the heart of the Phantom. The casting team initially considered a range of actresses, including some who were already established in the musical theater world. Names like Emmy Rossum, who ultimately secured the role, were in the mix alongside others like Anne Hathaway and even Scarlett Johansson. Each of these actresses brought something unique to the table. Hathaway, with her Broadway pedigree and vocal prowess, could have delivered a performance filled with both vulnerability and strength, while Johansson's sultry voice and captivating presence would have added a different layer to Christine's character. However, Rossum's youthful innocence and remarkable vocal talent ultimately won over the casting directors, making her portrayal memorable and beloved.

And let's not forget Raoul, the dashing viscount who serves as Christine's love interest. The casting choices here were equally intriguing. At one point, the filmmakers considered actors like Josh Hartnett and even the charming Hugh Jackman. Hartnett, with his brooding looks, might have brought a different kind of intensity to Raoul, while Jackman, known for his stage presence and charm, could have delivered a performance that balanced both the romantic and the heroic. However, the role eventually went to Patrick Wilson, whose portrayal struck a chord with audiences, showcasing Raoul's loyalty and determination.

The ensemble cast also had its share of interesting casting choices. For instance, the role of Madame Giry, the enigmatic ballet mistress, was originally rumored to be offered to seasoned actresses like Meryl Streep or even Judi Dench. Both would have brought a wealth of experience and gravitas to the character, yet the role ultimately went to Minnie Driver, who infused it with a unique blend of authority and maternal instinct.

As we delve deeper into the casting process, it becomes evident that the choices made were not just about star power; they were about finding the right fit for the story and the characters. The original casting choices reveal a landscape of missed opportunities and what-ifs, but they also highlight the serendipity of the final selections. Each actor brought their own interpretation and flair, weaving together a narrative that resonated with audiences around the world.

In hindsight, the original casting choices for "The Phantom of the Opera" serve as a reminder of how a film can evolve through the lens of its characters. The right actor can breathe life into a role, transforming a script into a living, breathing entity. While we may wonder what could have been with different casting choices, the final product stands as a testament to the magic of cinema and the enduring power of storytelling.

Behind the Ruby Slippers: Uncovering the Surprising Stories of 'The Wizard of Oz' Casting Process

When we think of the timeless classic "The Wizard of Oz," our minds often drift to the iconic performances of Judy Garland as Dorothy, Bert Lahr as the Cowardly Lion, and Jack Haley as the Tin Man. However, the path to casting these legendary roles was anything but straightforward. The original casting choices reveal a fascinating glimpse into Hollywood's past, filled with ambition, competition, and the ever-elusive quest for the perfect fit.

Let's start with the role of Dorothy. Before Judy Garland was selected, the studio had a different vision. The original choice for Dorothy was actually Shirley Temple, a child star adored by audiences for her charm and talent. However, Temple's contractual obligations with 20th Century Fox made it impossible for her to take on the role. Imagine a world where Dorothy clicked her heels in those famous ruby slippers while singing "Over the Rainbow" with Temple's sweet voice. It's a tantalizing thought, but fate had other plans. After Temple, the studio considered other actresses, including Deanna Durbin and even a young actress named Margaret O'Brien. Ultimately, Judy Garland, who had been struggling to find her footing in the industry, was cast. Her portrayal not only became iconic but also transformed her career, solidifying her status as a Hollywood legend.

Now, let's talk about the Cowardly Lion. Originally, the role was intended for the talented actor and singer, Bert Lahr, but the producers were initially interested in a more established star: W.C. Fields. Fields was a comedic genius known for his distinctive voice and larger-than-life persona. However, his reputation for being difficult and his penchant for alcohol led to concerns about his reliability on set. Lahr, on the other hand, brought a unique blend of vulnerability and humor to the character, ultimately making him the perfect choice. His performance, complete with a memorable rendition of "If I Only Had the Nerve," left an indelible mark on the film and audiences alike.

Then, we have the Tin Man. The role was originally offered to Buddy Ebsen, a talented dancer and actor known for his energetic performances. Ebsen was excited about the prospect of playing the Tin Man, but fate intervened once again. During the early stages of production, he suffered a severe allergic reaction to the aluminum dust used in the makeup for the character. This unfortunate incident forced him to withdraw from the project, and the role eventually went to Jack Haley, who was able to wear a different makeup formula that didn't cause him any health issues. Haley's portrayal brought warmth and humor to the Tin Man, and his heartfelt rendition of "If I Only Had a Heart" became one of the film's most memorable moments.

The casting of the Scarecrow also had its share of twists. Initially, the role was offered to the beloved comedian and actor, Ray Bolger. However, Bolger had his sights set on the Tin Man and was initially reluctant to take on the Scarecrow. The studio, eager to have him on board, eventually convinced him to embrace the role, and he brought an endearing charm and physicality that made the Scarecrow one of the film's standout characters. Bolger's performance, coupled with his iconic dance sequences, showcased his incredible talent and solidified the Scarecrow's place in cinematic history.

The original casting choices for "The Wizard of Oz" highlight the unpredictable nature of filmmaking. What could have been a very different film with different actors ultimately became a beloved classic, transcending generations. Each actor brought their unique flair to their roles, creating a magical tapestry that continues to enchant audiences worldwide. The journey of casting this film serves as a reminder that sometimes, the most unexpected paths lead to the most extraordinary destinations. In the end, it was the chemistry, the talent, and the serendipity of those chosen that created the enchanting world of Oz, forever etched in the hearts of fans.

Apocalypse Now's Turbulent Casting History Revealed: From Steve McQueen to Martin Sheen

When discussing the iconic film "Apocalypse Now," directed by Francis Ford Coppola, one must delve into its tumultuous production history, especially the original casting choices that shaped the vision of this cinematic masterpiece. The film, released in 1979, is often hailed as one of the greatest films ever made, but the journey to its final cast was fraught with challenges and unexpected turns.

Initially, the role of Captain Benjamin Willard was intended for the legendary actor, Steve McQueen. McQueen, with his rugged charm and intense screen presence, seemed like a perfect fit for the role of a haunted soldier tasked with a morally ambiguous mission in the heart of the Vietnam War. However, McQueen had his own vision for the character, which included altering the script to suit his interpretation. This creative clash led to a parting of ways, as Coppola sought a different actor who could embody the character's psychological depth without the complications of extensive rewrites.

Next in line was the rising star of the time, Al Pacino. Pacino had just come off the success of "The Godfather," and his intense performances were captivating audiences everywhere. However, as fate would have it, Pacino was unable to commit to the project due to scheduling conflicts. His absence was a significant blow, as many believed he could have brought a unique energy to Willard. The search continued, and the role eventually fell to Martin Sheen, who, at the time, was not as widely recognized but had a raw talent that resonated with Coppola's vision. Sheen's portrayal of Willard became iconic, infused with a sense of desperation and moral ambiguity that perfectly captured the film's themes.

Then there was the character of Colonel Walter Kurtz, originally envisioned for the enigmatic Jack Nicholson. Nicholson's ability to portray complex and unhinged characters made him a prime candidate for the role of the rogue colonel who had descended into madness. However, Nicholson's commitment to other projects meant that he could not take on the role, leading Coppola to consider other actors. The director ultimately cast Marlon Brando, a choice that would become one of the film's most memorable aspects. Brando, despite his notorious reputation for being difficult on set, brought an unparalleled gravitas to Kurtz, delivering lines that echoed with philosophical depth. His portrayal was haunting, and the film's climax hinged on the chilling interaction between Willard and Kurtz.

Another interesting casting consideration was for the role of Lieutenant Colonel Bill Kilgore. The character, known for his love of surfing and his cavalier attitude toward war, was originally offered to the charismatic and versatile actor, Robert Duvall. Duvall, who would eventually take on the role, infused Kilgore with a sense of bravado and dark humor that became iconic. His famous line about the smell of napalm in the morning encapsulated the film's juxtaposition of beauty and horror, a theme that resonates throughout the narrative.

Moreover, the casting process was not just about the lead roles. The film featured a remarkable ensemble, including Dennis Hopper as the photojournalist, a character that was originally intended for other actors. Hopper's unpredictable energy and improvisational skills brought a chaotic brilliance to the film, enhancing its surreal atmosphere. The ensemble cast was a reflection of Coppola's desire to create a sense of authenticity amidst the madness of war.

In retrospect, the casting choices for "Apocalypse Now" illustrate the unpredictability of filmmaking. The original intentions may have shifted dramatically, but the final selections resulted in an unforgettable portrayal of the human condition amidst the horrors of war. Each actor brought their unique flair, contributing to a film that continues to resonate with audiences. The journey of casting "Apocalypse Now" serves as a testament to the creative process, where the unexpected can lead to extraordinary outcomes, ultimately crafting a narrative that is both timeless and haunting.

The 'Goodfellas' That Never Was: Alternate Choices for Liotta, De Niro, and Pesci

When you think about the classic film "Goodfellas," directed by Martin Scorsese, it's hard not to envision the iconic performances that brought the characters to life. Ray Liotta as Henry Hill, Robert De Niro as Jimmy Conway, and Joe Pesci as Tommy DeVito have become synonymous with the film, but the casting process was anything but straightforward. In fact, the original choices for these roles could have led to a very different interpretation of this mobster epic.

Let's start with Henry Hill, the character at the center of this crime saga. Initially, the role was eyed by several actors before Ray Liotta ultimately secured it. One of the prominent names in consideration was Johnny Depp. At the time, Depp was rising in Hollywood, known for his work in "21 Jump Street" and "Edward Scissorhands." His unique charisma and ability to portray complex characters could have lent a different flavor to Henry Hill. However, his schedule and the nature of the character may have ultimately led to the decision to pass. Another actor who was considered was Matthew Modine, who had gained recognition from films like "Full Metal Jacket." Modine's intensity could have brought a different depth to Hill's character, but perhaps he lacked the raw edge that Liotta ultimately delivered.

Then we have Jimmy Conway, the shrewd and calculating mobster played by Robert De Niro. Interestingly, De Niro was not the first choice for this role either. The filmmakers initially considered the legendary Al Pacino. Imagine Pacino's iconic delivery and intense presence in this role, bringing his unique flair to the character. However, Pacino was already deeply involved in other projects and ultimately turned it down. Another name floated around was the talented actor, Eric Roberts. Known for his roles in "Runaway Train" and "The Pope of Greenwich Village," Roberts had the acting chops but lacked the gravitas that De Niro brought to the role, making it a pivotal moment in the film's casting history.

Now, let's talk about Tommy DeVito, the volatile and unpredictable character that Joe Pesci immortalized. Pesci's performance earned him an Academy Award for Best Supporting Actor, but he wasn't the only actor considered for this explosive role. Initially, the filmmakers looked at other actors, including the late John Turturro. Turturro's ability to blend humor and intensity could have created a fascinating take on Tommy, but it's hard to imagine anyone else delivering the same level of raw ferocity and dark comedy that Pesci did. Another actor in the mix was Steven Bauer, who had made a name for himself in "Scarface." Bauer's charm and intensity could have brought a different energy to the character, but again, it's Pesci's unique blend of menace and hilarity that truly defined Tommy DeVito.

As the casting process unfolded, Scorsese and producer Irwin Winkler found themselves navigating a complex web of personalities and schedules. The chemistry between the actors was also a crucial factor. The trio of Liotta, De Niro, and Pesci created a dynamic that was electric on screen, and it's hard to envision how the film would have fared had any of the original choices landed those roles.

In hindsight, the casting of "Goodfellas" is a testament to the unpredictability of filmmaking. The choices made during casting can shape the entire narrative, and in this case, the final selections were nothing short of perfect. Each actor brought their own unique interpretation to the roles, creating a film that has stood the test of time. The journey of casting "Goodfellas" reminds us that sometimes, the stars align in the most unexpected ways, leading to cinematic magic that resonates with audiences for generations. It's a fascinating glimpse into the behind-the-scenes decisions that ultimately crafted one of the greatest films in American cinema history.

From Depp to Pitt: The Surprising Casting Decisions That Shaped "Fight Club"'s Legacy

When we think of iconic films, "Fight Club" often rises to the top of the list, not just for its provocative themes and unforgettable lines, but also for its casting choices that have become synonymous with the characters themselves. However, the journey to the final casting of this cult classic was anything but straightforward. The original casting choices reveal a fascinating glimpse into how different the film could have been. It's a story of near-misses, unexpected turns, and the serendipity of Hollywood.

Initially, the role of the Narrator, the unnamed protagonist who struggles with insomnia and identity, was offered to none other than Johnny Depp. Imagine that for a moment. Depp, with his penchant for quirky and offbeat characters, could have brought an entirely different flavor to the role. The idea of a charismatic, yet deeply troubled figure portrayed by Depp is intriguing, but ultimately, he turned it down. Instead, the role went to Edward Norton, whose performance became a defining moment in his career. Norton's ability to convey vulnerability while simultaneously embodying the darker aspects of the character made him the perfect fit.

Then there's the character of Tyler Durden, the enigmatic soap salesman who becomes the Narrator's alter ego. Initially, the filmmakers had their eyes set on Brad Pitt, who eventually did land the role, but the road to that decision was winding. At one point, David Fincher, the director, considered casting Matt Damon. Damon, known for his boy-next-door charm, would have brought a different energy to Tyler. The idea of him as the rebellious figure who incites the Narrator's transformation is a curious thought, as the character is meant to be both alluring and dangerous. Ultimately, the decision to cast Pitt was pivotal. His charisma and physicality brought Tyler to life in a way that resonated with audiences, making him a cultural icon.

The supporting characters also had their share of near-casting decisions. Marla Singer, the love interest and catalyst for much of the Narrator's turmoil, was originally intended for a different actress. While Helena Bonham Carter ultimately delivered a performance that was raw and captivating, the role was briefly considered for Reese Witherspoon. Witherspoon, at the time, was known for her roles in romantic comedies and had yet to fully embrace the edgier, darker characters that would come later in her career. Imagining Marla with her bubbly persona is a stark contrast to the chaotic energy Carter brought to the screen, making one realize how crucial the right casting can be in shaping a character's identity.

And let's not forget about the role of Robert Paulsen, the tragic figure whose mantra of "His name is Robert Paulsen" resonates throughout the film. Originally, the filmmakers had thought about casting a more conventional actor for the role. However, it was Meat Loaf who ultimately brought depth to the character, transforming Paulsen into a symbol of the struggle against the dehumanizing aspects of consumer culture. Meat Loaf's physical presence and emotional performance added layers to the character that a different choice might not have achieved.

The casting process for "Fight Club" is a testament to the unpredictable nature of filmmaking. Each decision, each near-miss, shaped the film into what it became. It's a reminder that the right actor can elevate a script, breathing life into words on a page and creating something that resonates with audiences for generations. The choices made, the actors who were considered, and the ones who ultimately stepped into those roles all played a part in crafting a film that challenges societal norms and invites viewers to question their own realities. In the end, "Fight Club" is not just a movie; it's a cultural phenomenon, and the casting choices are integral to its legacy.

The Surprising Choices Behind the Iconic Cast of 'Alien'

When we think of the 1979 science fiction horror film "Alien," we often picture Sigourney Weaver as the iconic Ellen Ripley, a character who would go on to redefine the role of women in action and horror films. However, the casting process for "Alien" was a labyrinthine journey filled with unexpected choices and fascinating backstories that could have altered the course of cinematic history. It's easy to overlook how pivotal casting decisions are in shaping the essence of a film, and "Alien" is no exception.

Originally, the role of Ripley was not a foregone conclusion for Weaver. In fact, the creative team behind "Alien," including director Ridley Scott and producer Walter Hill, initially considered a different approach to the character. They were looking for someone who could embody both strength and vulnerability, but the first choices for the role were far from the eventual casting. Among the early contenders were actresses like Meryl Streep, who was just beginning to make her mark in Hollywood. Streep's talent was undeniable, but the filmmakers were uncertain whether her dramatic gravitas would translate into the sci-fi horror genre.

Then there was the consideration of Anne Bancroft, known for her powerful performances in films like "The Graduate." Bancroft was a respected actress with a commanding presence, but the role of Ripley required a unique blend of toughness and relatability that was harder to capture in her established persona. The casting team also looked at various models and actresses who were more traditionally associated with the genre, but none seemed to have the right combination of qualities that would resonate with audiences in the way they envisioned.

Meanwhile, the character of Dallas, the ship's captain, was initially meant for a different kind of actor as well. The role was originally offered to the legendary actor Jack Nicholson, who was coming off a string of iconic performances. However, Nicholson's star power and larger-than-life persona posed a challenge for the film's tone. Ridley Scott wanted someone who could bring a sense of realism to the role, and thus he turned to Tom Skerritt, who would ultimately bring a more grounded and relatable quality to Dallas, allowing the audience to connect with the crew's harrowing experience in deep space.

Interestingly, the casting of other crew members also went through a series of transformations. The role of Ash, the ship's science officer, was originally eyed for more established actors like Ian Holm, but the filmmakers were also considering less conventional choices. The idea of casting a young, relatively unknown actor was a gamble that ultimately paid off, as Holm's portrayal of Ash became one of the film's most chilling elements. His transformation from a seemingly benign crew member to a sinister android was a highlight of the narrative, showcasing the film's ability to subvert expectations.

The character of Lambert, played by Veronica Cartwright, was also a point of contention during casting discussions. Originally, the filmmakers had considered several prominent actresses, including the likes of Shelley Duvall. However, they ultimately decided to go with Cartwright, who brought a unique blend of vulnerability and strength to the role. Her performance resonated with audiences, adding to the film's dynamic portrayal of fear and survival.

In the end, the casting of "Alien" came together in a way that no one could have predicted. The final ensemble, including Weaver, Skerritt, Holm, and Cartwright, created a chemistry that elevated the film beyond its genre roots. The choices made during the casting process were not just about finding the right actors; they were about shaping the very fabric of the story itself. The original casting choices, while intriguing, ultimately paved the way for a film that would not only terrify audiences but also leave an indelible mark on the landscape of science fiction and horror. It's a testament to the power of collaboration and the serendipitous nature of filmmaking, where every decision can lead to the creation of something iconic.

A Peek at 'A Clockwork Orange's Alternate Casting Choices

When we delve into the world of cinema, we often find ourselves captivated by the final product, the polished performances, the carefully crafted scenes, and the mesmerizing storytelling. Yet, behind every iconic film lies a labyrinth of decisions, a web of choices that often go unnoticed. Take, for instance, the cult classic "A Clockwork Orange," directed by Stanley Kubrick and released in 1971. This film, based on Anthony Burgess's novel, is a striking commentary on free will, violence, and societal control. However, what many may not realize is the fascinating journey of its casting choices, a journey that could have led to a very different interpretation of this provocative narrative.

Initially, the role of Alex DeLarge, the film's notorious protagonist, was not destined for Malcolm McDowell, whose performance would ultimately become legendary. Before McDowell's name emerged, Kubrick had considered a variety of actors, each bringing their own unique flair, yet none quite resonated with the director's vision. One of the most notable names that surfaced in the casting discussions was that of David Hemmings, known for his role in "Blow-Up." Hemmings had the youth and the rebellious spirit that Kubrick sought, but ultimately, the director felt that he lacked the necessary edge to embody the chilling complexity of Alex.

Another contender was the enigmatic actor and musician, Michael Gothard. With his striking features and intense presence, Gothard seemed a fitting choice. However, as the casting process unfolded, it became clear that his interpretation of Alex leaned more towards the brooding and less towards the charismatic sociopath that Kubrick envisioned. The director was searching for someone who could evoke both charm and menace, a delicate balance that would keep audiences both enthralled and horrified.

Interestingly, the casting process also opened the door for the idea of a more established star. The name of the legendary actor, Robert Redford, floated through the casting discussions for a brief moment. Redford, with his all-American charm and bankable star power, could have brought a different dimension to the character. However, Kubrick's vision was to challenge the audience, to provoke thought and discomfort. Redford, despite his undeniable talent, was too closely associated with heroism and virtue, qualities that stood in stark contrast to the morally ambiguous world of "A Clockwork Orange."

As the search continued, the name of Jon Voight emerged, a rising star who had just gained acclaim for his role in "Midnight Cowboy." Voight's ability to convey vulnerability and toughness made him a strong candidate. However, he ultimately declined the role, feeling that the character was too far removed from his own sensibilities. This decision paved the way for McDowell, who, at the time, was relatively unknown but had already made a name for himself in British cinema. His audition was a revelation; he embodied Alex with a ferocity and charisma that captivated Kubrick. McDowell brought an unsettling charm to the role, making audiences question their own moral compass as they watched him revel in chaos.

The casting of the other characters was equally intriguing. For the role of the Cat Lady, Kubrick initially considered a range of actresses, including the talented but unconventional Glenda Jackson. Ultimately, the choice fell to the lesser-known but equally compelling actress, Miriam Karlin, whose performance added layers to the film's exploration of violence and vulnerability.

In retrospect, the original casting choices for "A Clockwork Orange" reveal a complex interplay of artistic vision and the unpredictable nature of film production. Each actor considered brought their own essence to the table, yet it was ultimately Malcolm McDowell's haunting portrayal that defined the film. The decisions made in the casting room shaped not just the characters but the very essence of the film itself, reminding us that the path to cinematic greatness is often paved with what could have been.

Exploring the Original Casting Choices for Butch Cassidy and the Sundance Kid

When we think of classic films, few titles resonate quite like "Butch Cassidy and the Sundance Kid." Released in 1969, it became an iconic representation of the Western genre, blending humor, adventure, and a touch of melancholy. However, the story of its casting is almost as fascinating as the film itself. Originally, the roles of Butch Cassidy and the Sundance Kid were intended for a different duo, one that would have changed the film's chemistry and legacy entirely.

Initially, the producers envisioned a pairing that was quite different from the eventual leads, Paul Newman and Robert Redford. The first choice for Butch Cassidy was none other than Steve McQueen, a superstar of the era known for his rugged charm and action-hero persona. McQueen's involvement would have brought a different energy to the character. His style was more aloof, more intense, and he had a certain rebelliousness that had captivated audiences in films like "The Great Escape" and "Bullitt." The producers believed his star power could draw in a larger audience, and they were not wrong about that. However, McQueen had other commitments, and the project was pushed back, creating a window for alternative casting.

Meanwhile, the role of the Sundance Kid was first offered to none other than Jack Lemmon. Now, Jack Lemmon is a legendary actor, known for his versatility and comedic timing. He had a knack for playing characters that were likable yet flawed, a perfect fit for the Sundance Kid, who was more of a sharpshooter with a heart. Yet, the chemistry between Lemmon and McQueen would have undoubtedly shifted the tone of the film. While Lemmon could have brought a unique charm and humor to the role, the dynamic would have leaned more towards a buddy-cop feel rather than the romanticized outlaw bond that Newman and Redford ultimately created.

As fate would have it, both McQueen and Lemmon turned down the roles. This opened the door for Paul Newman, who was initially hesitant about taking on Butch Cassidy. Newman had an established career and was known for his dramatic roles, but he was also drawn to the opportunity to explore the humor inherent in the character. With a little persuasion, he accepted the role, bringing his signature charisma and depth to Butch.

Then came Robert Redford, who was not the first choice for Sundance either. The casting team had their eye on a variety of actors, including Warren Beatty and even the now-legendary Burt Reynolds. However, Redford's audition was a revelation. He brought a youthful exuberance and a certain vulnerability to the role that was impossible to ignore. His chemistry with Newman was electric, creating a dynamic that resonated with audiences and critics alike. They had a brotherly bond that felt genuine, elevating the film beyond a simple Western into a poignant exploration of friendship and loyalty.

The film's success can be attributed not only to its writing and direction but also to this serendipitous casting. Newman and Redford became synonymous with their roles, and their performances defined the film. They managed to balance humor with the weight of their characters' eventual fate, creating a lasting impact on the genre and cinema as a whole.

Reflecting on the original casting choices, it's intriguing to consider how different the film could have been. Would McQueen's intensity have overshadowed the lightheartedness of the script? Would Lemmon's comedic style have clashed with the film's more serious undertones? It's a fascinating exercise in what-ifs, but ultimately, the universe aligned perfectly for "Butch Cassidy and the Sundance Kid."

The legacy of this film is not just in its storytelling or its beautiful cinematography; it lies in the perfect pairing of Newman and Redford, a duo that became legends in their own right, forever immortalized in cinematic history.

From Billy Crystal to Tom Hanks: The Fascinating Journey of Toy Story's Casting

When we think of the iconic film "Toy Story," it's hard not to picture the beloved characters that have become staples of animated cinema. Woody, Buzz Lightyear, and the ensemble of toys have captured the hearts of audiences worldwide. However, the journey to casting these characters was filled with fascinating choices that could have led the film down an entirely different path. The original casting choices for "Toy Story" offer a glimpse into what might have been, and it's a story worth telling.

Initially, Tom Hanks was not the first choice for the role of Woody. In fact, the character was originally intended to be voiced by the legendary comedian and actor, Billy Crystal. Crystal was a popular figure at the time, known for his sharp wit and comedic timing. The creative team behind "Toy Story" envisioned Woody as a charming, albeit slightly sarcastic character, and they believed Crystal could bring that essence to life. However, as the project developed, Crystal ultimately passed on the role, feeling that the character was not quite right for him. This decision opened the door for Tom Hanks, who would go on to embody Woody with such warmth and depth that it's hard to imagine anyone else in the role. Hanks brought a unique blend of humor and heart, transforming Woody into a character that resonated with both children and adults alike.

Now, let's talk about Buzz Lightyear. The character of Buzz was originally intended to be voiced by none other than the charismatic actor, Jim Carrey. At the time, Carrey was riding high on the success of films like "Ace Ventura: Pet Detective" and "The Mask." His high-energy style seemed like a perfect match for the over-the-top space ranger. However, as the casting process unfolded, the filmmakers realized that Buzz needed a different kind of voice—one that could balance bravado with vulnerability. This led them to cast Tim Allen, who was known for his stand-up comedy and his hit television show "Home Improvement." Allen's portrayal of Buzz Lightyear brought a layered complexity to the character, allowing audiences to see both the bravado of a space hero and the insecurities of a toy trying to find his place in the world.

The ensemble cast of "Toy Story" also underwent some intriguing changes. For instance, the role of Mr. Potato Head was originally offered to the legendary comedian Don Rickles. Rickles was known for his sharp tongue and quick wit, making him an ideal candidate for the wisecracking toy. However, Rickles was initially hesitant about the role, fearing that his style of humor might not translate well in an animated format. Eventually, he was convinced to take on the role, and his performance became one of the film's highlights, adding a layer of humor that perfectly complemented the other characters.

Another interesting casting choice was for the character of Rex, the timid dinosaur. Originally, the filmmakers considered casting the late, great actor and comedian, John Candy, for the role. Candy's ability to convey warmth and humor would have brought a different flavor to Rex, but sadly, Candy passed away before the project could move forward. Ultimately, the role went to Wallace Shawn, whose distinctive voice and ability to portray vulnerability gave Rex a unique charm that audiences adored.

As we reflect on the original casting choices for "Toy Story," it becomes clear that these decisions significantly shaped the film's legacy. Each actor brought their unique talents to their roles, creating a rich tapestry of characters that continue to resonate with audiences today.

The film not only set the stage for a new era of animation but also demonstrated the power of collaboration and the importance of finding the right voice for each character. The journey of casting "Toy Story" serves as a reminder that sometimes, the best choices emerge from unexpected circumstances, leading to a masterpiece that stands the test of time.

Die Hard's Intriguing Cast Alternatives and the Roadmap to Bruce Willis' Triumph

When you think of iconic action films, "Die Hard" undoubtedly comes to mind. Released in 1988, it's become a staple of the genre, but what if I told you that the casting choices were almost entirely different? Imagine a world where the characters we know and love were portrayed by completely different actors. The film, directed by John McTiernan, has a legacy that has influenced countless action films since, but the journey to casting the lead role of John McClane was anything but straightforward.

Initially, the role of John McClane was offered to a variety of actors, some of whom might surprise you. One of the first choices was actually Frank Sinatra. Yes, you heard that right. Sinatra was offered the role because he had starred in the film "The Detective," which was based on the same source material as "Die Hard." However, Sinatra was in his seventies at the time, and the idea of him running around a skyscraper, battling terrorists, was a bit far-fetched. Thankfully, he declined, paving the way for a more suitable candidate.

Next up was Arnold Schwarzenegger. At the peak of his action-hero status, Schwarzenegger was a household name, known for his roles in films like "The Terminator" and "Predator." Just imagine him as McClane, delivering one-liners while taking down terrorists. However, he was busy filming "Red Heat," and his commitment to that project meant he couldn't take on the role in "Die Hard." The producers were looking for someone with a blend of action and relatability, someone who could embody the everyman caught in extraordinary circumstances.

Then came the suggestion of a young and rising star, Bruce Willis. At that time, Willis was primarily known for his role in the television series "Moonlighting." He was an unconventional choice for an action hero; he wasn't the muscular, tough-guy archetype that Hollywood often favored. However, the producers saw something in him—an ability to balance humor with grit. He had that charm, that wit, and most importantly, he could portray vulnerability. After a screen test, which was met with enthusiasm, Willis was ultimately cast as John McClane, and the rest, as they say, is history.

But the casting choices didn't stop there. The role of Hans Gruber, the film's antagonist, was initially offered to several notable actors. The legendary actor Al Pacino was considered for the role, but he turned it down, feeling that the character was not compelling enough. Can you imagine Pacino's intense energy and charisma as Gruber? It's fascinating to think about how different the film might have been with him in that role. Eventually, the part went to Alan Rickman, who delivered a performance that remains one of the most memorable villain portrayals in cinematic history. Rickman brought a sophisticated menace to Gruber that was both chilling and captivating, and his unique accent and delivery added layers to the character.

The supporting cast also saw its share of interesting choices. The role of Holly Gennaro, McClane's estranged wife, was initially considered for actresses like Sharon Stone and even Jennifer Jason Leigh. Ultimately, it went to Bonnie Bedelia, who brought a strong presence to the role, complementing Willis's portrayal of McClane perfectly.

As we look back at the original casting choices for "Die Hard," it's clear that the film could have taken a very different direction. The chemistry between Willis and Rickman, the humor interspersed with action, and the relatable everyman hero are all elements that have become defining features of the film. The casting decisions, which might have seemed unconventional at the time, ultimately contributed to the film's success and its enduring legacy as a holiday classic and a benchmark for action films. It's a reminder of how pivotal casting can be in shaping not just a film, but an entire genre.

The Chosen Ones: How William H. Macy, Frances McDormand, and Steve Buscemi Brought Life to the Coen Brothers' "Fargo"

When we think of the Coen brothers' iconic film "Fargo," it's hard to separate the story from the unforgettable performances that brought it to life. The film, released in 1996, is a masterclass in blending dark comedy with crime drama, and its characters are etched in the minds of audiences everywhere. But before Frances McDormand donned the badge of Marge Gunderson, or William H. Macy became Jerry Lundegaard, there were other names in the mix—casting choices that could have dramatically shifted the tone and reception of the film.

Initially, the Coen brothers had a very different vision for their leading characters. They envisioned a more traditional approach to casting, with names that would carry weight and recognition. For Marge Gunderson, the role that ultimately won McDormand an Academy Award, the Coens considered several actresses who were more established at the time. Among those names were Holly Hunter and Jennifer Jason Leigh. Both were at the height of their careers, with Hunter known for her strong performances in films like "The Piano" and Leigh making waves with her roles in "Single White Female" and "The Hateful Eight." The Coens were drawn to their talent but ultimately felt they wouldn't quite capture the unique blend of warmth and tenacity that McDormand brought to the role.

The casting process for Jerry Lundegaard was equally intriguing. Initially, the Coen brothers had their sights set on Steve Buscemi for the role, but they also considered actors like John C. Reilly and even the late, great Philip Seymour Hoffman. Each of these actors had their own distinct styles and approaches, which could have led to a different interpretation of Jerry's desperate, bumbling character. The Coens, however, ultimately decided on William H. Macy, whose portrayal of Jerry's ineptitude and moral decay became one of the film's standout performances. Macy's ability to evoke both sympathy and frustration made Jerry a complex character, and it's fascinating to think how the film might have shifted had a different actor taken the role.

Then there's the character of Carl Showalter, the ruthless hitman played by Steve Buscemi. The Coens initially considered casting the likes of Tim Roth or even Johnny Depp, both of whom had the chops to bring a quirky yet menacing energy to the character. However, they ultimately settled on Buscemi, whose unique physicality and vocal delivery brought a level of unpredictability that became integral to the film's tension. The chemistry between Buscemi and his co-star, Peter Stormare, who played Gaear Grimsrud, became one of the film's highlights, creating an eerie yet darkly comedic dynamic that would have felt different with other actors.

Let's not forget about the supporting characters, either. The role of Norm Gunderson, Marge's husband, was initially considered for actors like John Goodman and Bruce Campbell. Goodman, with his imposing presence and comedic timing, could have offered a different take on the supportive yet understated husband, while Campbell's cult status might have brought a unique flair to the character. Ultimately, the Coens chose to go with John Carroll Lynch, whose subtle performance added depth and authenticity to the film's portrayal of domestic life in Minnesota.

The casting choices in "Fargo" are a testament to the Coen brothers' vision and their understanding of character dynamics. Each actor brought something unique to their roles, creating a cohesive yet diverse ensemble that elevated the narrative. The film is a reminder of how casting can shape a story, and looking back at the original choices offers a fascinating glimpse into what might have been. The Coens' final selections not only defined the characters but also contributed to the film's legacy as a cult classic, one that continues to resonate with audiences today. In the end, it's the chemistry, the unexpected choices, and the bold performances that make "Fargo" a timeless piece of cinema, forever etched in the annals of film history.

The Alternate "Breakfast Club": What Could Have Been if Hughes Had Chosen Differently

When we think of iconic films from the 1980s, "The Breakfast Club" inevitably comes to mind. It's a movie that transcends generations, capturing the essence of teenage angst, friendship, and the struggle for identity. But what if I told you that the casting choices we know today were not the original vision of director John Hughes? The story behind the casting of this film is almost as fascinating as the film itself, and it reveals the complexities of Hollywood during that era.

Initially, Hughes had a different lineup in mind for the five central characters who would come to represent the quintessential high school archetypes. The role of the brain, Brian Johnson, was originally offered to the talented actor Anthony Michael Hall, who ultimately did secure the part. Hall brought a depth to Brian that resonated with audiences, but he wasn't the only one considered. Hughes had also eyed other young actors, including a then-unknown Tom Cruise, who was on the cusp of stardom. Can you imagine Cruise in that role, with his trademark charm and intensity? It's a stark contrast to Hall's more subdued and relatable portrayal.

Next, we have the character of the princess, Claire Standish. Originally, Hughes envisioned a different actress altogether. Before Molly Ringwald was cast, the role was offered to actress and model Jennifer Beals, who had gained fame for her role in "Flashdance." Beals was undoubtedly a rising star, and her involvement would have brought a different energy to the character. However, Beals turned it down, and that opened the door for Ringwald, who infused Claire with a mix of vulnerability and strength. Ringwald's performance became emblematic of the film, and it's hard to imagine anyone else in that role.

Then there's the character of the rebel, John Bender. The original casting choice for Bender was none other than the brooding actor Rob Lowe. Lowe was known for his good looks and charm, but he was also a versatile actor capable of portraying the complexities of a troubled teen. However, Lowe was busy with other commitments and couldn't take on the role. Enter Judd Nelson, who brought a raw, edgy energy to Bender that has since become iconic. Nelson's portrayal of the rebellious teen was filled with a mix of anger and vulnerability, and it's this performance that many fans remember most vividly.

The character of the athlete, Andrew Clark, was initially considered for actor Emilio Estevez, who ultimately did land the role. Estevez's performance as the jock with hidden insecurities resonated with audiences, but interestingly enough, Hughes had also thought about casting a different actor: Charlie Sheen. Sheen was already making a name for himself in Hollywood, and while he would have brought a different vibe to the character, Estevez's portrayal added layers to Andrew that made him relatable and human.

Finally, there's the character of Allison Reynolds, the outcast. Originally, Hughes had his sights set on casting actress Ally Sheedy. Sheedy did eventually get the role, but it's worth noting that Hughes had considered other actresses as well, including Winona Ryder. Ryder, who would go on to become a major star, might have brought a different interpretation to the quirky character of Allison. Yet, Sheedy's performance, with its subtle nuances and emotional depth, became a defining aspect of the film.

The casting of "The Breakfast Club" is a testament to the unpredictable nature of filmmaking. Each actor brought their unique flair, transforming the characters into unforgettable icons of teen cinema. The original choices may have created an entirely different film, but it's the chemistry and talent of the final cast that made "The Breakfast Club" a timeless classic. As we look back on this film, we can appreciate not just the performances but also the serendipity of casting that shaped a generation's understanding of adolescence.

Love, Chaos, and Cameron's Crisis: The Wild Adventures of 'Ferris Bueller's Day Off' Casting

When you think of "Ferris Bueller's Day Off," the iconic image of Matthew Broderick as Ferris, charming his way through a day of adventure in Chicago, immediately comes to mind. But what if I told you that the casting of this beloved character could have looked entirely different? The film, released in 1986 and directed by John Hughes, has become a cultural touchstone, but the journey to finding the right Ferris was anything but straightforward.

Initially, the role of Ferris Bueller was offered to another actor, someone who was already a household name in the mid-1980s. Can you imagine a world where Ferris was portrayed by none other than John Cusack? Cusack was a rising star, known for his roles in films like "Sixteen Candles" and "Better Off Dead." He had that quintessential charm and wit that could have easily brought Ferris to life. However, Cusack turned down the role, citing concerns about being typecast in a comedic role. This decision opened the door for Broderick, who had already made a name for himself on Broadway and was eager to make his mark in film.

Another interesting casting choice was the character of Cameron Frye, Ferris's best friend. Initially, the role was offered to Anthony Michael Hall, who had already worked with Hughes on "The Breakfast Club." Hall was known for his quirky, nerdy characters, and while he was undoubtedly talented, he ultimately passed on the role, feeling that he needed to explore different avenues in his career. This led to the casting of Alan Ruck, who brought a unique vulnerability and depth to Cameron, perfectly embodying the character's internal struggles and fears. Ruck's performance became one of the film's highlights, showcasing the tension between Ferris's carefree attitude and Cameron's anxiety.

And then there's Sloane Peterson, the love interest who captured Ferris's heart. The role was originally considered for a few actresses, including Jennifer Grey, who had just starred in "Dirty Dancing." However, the film's production team felt that Grey's rising fame might overshadow the character of Sloane, leading them to look elsewhere. Ultimately, they found Mia Sara, whose portrayal of Sloane was both charming and captivating. Sara brought a sense of authenticity to the role, making Sloane not just a pretty face but a strong character in her own right, someone who could hold her own alongside Ferris and Cameron.

One of the most fascinating aspects of the casting process was the decision for the character of Ed Rooney, the strict principal determined to catch Ferris in the act. The role was initially offered to a few different actors, including the legendary actor and comedian, Bill Murray. Can you imagine Murray as the no-nonsense principal? While he would have undoubtedly brought his unique comedic flair to the role, Murray ultimately declined, believing that the character needed a more straightforward approach. This led to the casting of Jeffrey Jones, whose portrayal of Rooney became iconic in its own right, perfectly balancing the character's absurdity with a sense of authority that made him both laughable and formidable.

As we reflect on these original casting choices, it's clear that the film we know and love could have taken a completely different shape. The chemistry between Broderick, Ruck, and Sara became a defining aspect of the film, creating a dynamic that resonated with audiences and solidified its status as a classic. The decisions made during the casting process not only shaped the film's narrative but also influenced the careers of the actors involved.

In the end, "Ferris Bueller's Day Off" is a testament to the idea that casting is not just about finding the right actor for a role; it's about creating a synergy that brings a story to life. The original choices may have been intriguing, but the final cast created a film that continues to inspire and entertain generations, reminding us all to take a day off and enjoy life.

The Road to Belushi: The Real Story of How the Cast of Animal House Was Shaped

When we think of classic comedies, few films stand out quite like "National Lampoon's Animal House." Released in 1978, it became a cultural touchstone, a defining moment in the genre of college comedies. But what many fans may not realize is that the path to the casting of this iconic film was anything but straightforward. The original casting choices are a fascinating story in their own right, filled with unexpected twists and turns that could have altered the very fabric of the film as we know it.

Initially, the role of Bluto Blutarsky, the unforgettable character played by John Belushi, was intended for a different actor. The filmmakers originally considered John Candy, a comedian known for his larger-than-life persona and improvisational skills. Candy had a unique charm that could have brought a different flavor to the character, but as fate would have it, he was ultimately unable to take on the role due to scheduling conflicts. This opened the door for Belushi, who was then a rising star on "Saturday Night Live." His portrayal of Bluto became legendary, a wild and reckless embodiment of college life that audiences still quote and remember fondly.

Then there was the character of Otter, originally envisioned for Chevy Chase. Chase, a well-known comedian at the time, had a distinct style that could have infused Otter with a different kind of charisma. However, due to his commitments to other projects, he too had to pass on the opportunity. This led to the casting of Tim Matheson, who brought his own unique interpretation to the role. Matheson's performance balanced the charm and mischief that Otter embodies, contributing to the film's overall dynamic.

The role of Flounder was originally offered to a different actor as well. The filmmakers had their eyes on a young and promising comedian named Peter Riegert, but he was not the only one in contention. The casting team also looked at several other actors, including a young and relatively unknown actor named Anthony Michael Hall, who would later become famous for his roles in John Hughes films. Ultimately, Riegert secured the part, and his portrayal of the lovable and awkward Flounder added a layer of depth to the ensemble.

The character of Dean Wormer, the stern authority figure, was originally considered for actor and comedian Alan Arkin. Arkin, known for his sharp wit and ability to play both comedic and serious roles, could have brought a different gravitas to Dean Wormer. However, the role eventually went to John Vernon, whose performance became iconic for its combination of humor and menace. Vernon's delivery of lines like "You're all worthless and weak!" has become a defining moment in the film, showcasing how casting choices can shape the tone and impact of a character.

Interestingly, the role of the sorority girl, who plays a pivotal part in the film's notorious party scenes, was initially offered to several actresses, including a young Goldie Hawn. However, due to various reasons, including her busy schedule and the film's unpredictable nature, she was unable to take the role. Instead, the filmmakers cast a lesser-known actress, who brought a fresh energy to the character, contributing to the film's chaotic atmosphere.

As we look back on "National Lampoon's Animal House," it's clear that the casting choices made during its development were crucial to its success. Each actor brought something unique to their roles, and the chemistry among the cast became a hallmark of the film. While we can only speculate how different choices might have altered the film's legacy, what remains undeniable is that the final ensemble created a perfect storm of comedy, chaos, and camaraderie that has resonated with audiences for decades. The original casting choices remind us that sometimes, the road to greatness is paved with unexpected detours, each leading to a destination that becomes iconic in its own right.

Also by Michael Pollick

Michael Pollick's Proving Ground
Michael Pollick's Proving Ground
The Keepinnit Reels
The Keepinnit Reels 2: Acoustic Boogaloo
The Zero Sugar Keepinnit Reels
Professor Mike's Low-Flow Fountain Of Information
A Wise Geek's Guide To Everything
A Wise Geek's Guide To Everything Volume 2
Professor Mike's Wealth Of Geeky Knowledge
Casting Conquests: The Surprising Runner-Ups for Iconic Roles